Truth By Name

Exploring Relationships between Sikhs and Christians

Truth By Name

Exploring Relationships between Sikhs and Christians

Tom Wilson

Copyright © 2022 Tom Wilson

Published in 2022 by Wide Margin,
90 Sandyleaze, Gloucester, GL2 0PX, UK
http://www.wide-margin.co.uk/

With grateful thanks to colleagues, both Sikh and Christian, for conversation, challenge and correction as we learn how to live well together.

The right of Tom Wilson to be identified as the Author of this Work has been asserted by him in accordance with the Copyright, Designs and Patents Act 1988.

All rights reserved. No part of this publication may be reproduced, stored in a retrieval system, or transmitted in any form or by any means electronic, or mechanical, photocopying, recording or otherwise, without the prior permission of the publisher or a licence permitting restricted copying.

ISBN 978-1-908860-08-8

Printed and bound in Great Britain by Lightning Source, Milton Keynes

Contents

1	Introduction	1
2	A Christian's thoughts about *Mul Mantar*	23
3	A Christian's Reflections on reading Japji	65
4	The *Janam Sakhis*	109
5	The five most popular *Janam Sakhis*	123
6	Sixth to Tenth Most Popular *Sakhis*	145
7	Other Important *Janam Sakhis*	161
8	Conversations between Christians and Sikhs	185
9	Sikhism and Christianity	203
10	Learning to Live Well Together	229

Chapter 1

Introduction

This book is an exercise in similarities and differences. I am writing as a committed Christian who is also committed to interfaith dialogue, that is, to explorations of how people of different faith and belief perspectives see and understand the world. I cannot call this book a conversation because no one else gets to speak. In a good conversation all those involved have the power to shape the direction and topic discussed; in writing this is not the case. I have done my best to engage with authors and texts on their own terms, but this is necessarily a subjective project, as it is centred on my perceptions and reactions to what others have written. It could be described as a monologue, but I hope it is one that stimulates the reader into asking questions and having further conversations with others.

Given the nature of the project, it is perhaps helpful to include some biographical information. My first prolonged encounters with those whose worldview is very different from my own came through studying Japanese in secondary school and then at university. This included six visits to Japan, varying in length from a few weeks to a year at a

INTRODUCTION

time. As I immersed myself in Japanese culture and adopted a Japanese lifestyle, it was clear to me that there are many, equally valid, ways of seeing the world. My academic engagement with faiths other than my own Christian faith began during my PhD, which explored Muslim experience of an Anglican primary school. I conducted ethnographic fieldwork amongst pupils and staff, and as a result of those two years became much more aware of my own subjectivity, as well as the importance of stating my own positionality when writing. I am a Christian, brought up in a Roman Catholic household and now ordained in the Anglican church, which is both Catholic and Reformed. My day job is running the St Philip's Centre, a Christian foundation interfaith training and resourcing Centre based in Leicester. Through my work at the Centre, especially in facilitating encounters between people of different faith and belief perspectives, I have often found it helpful to begin conversations about similarities and differences through textual encounter. Sitting with and speaking about the written word provides some degree of objectivity on which to base our subjective discussions of our own understandings of life and faith. One reason for writing is to provide a useful resource for Sikhs and Christians to have conversations that develop relationships of understanding, trust and cooperation.

My knowledge of the Sikh way of life is very limited, and I have written this book, in part, as a way of learning more. There are doubtless errors and omissions, for which I remain solely responsible. But I hope there are also interesting points of connection and dissonance, which will be useful for Sikhs and Christians who want to talk with each other about what they believe and how it shapes their daily lives.

Terminology is always a challenge in interfaith dialogue, not least because words mean different things to different adherents of the same faith, never mind conversations about the same word that are held between people of different faiths. A particularly challenging area of vocabulary is in reference to the divine; the English word "God" often carries implicit Christian and/or patriarchal assumptions. Sikhs refer to *Akal Purakh* (the Creator), *Waheguru*, the divine or the Supreme Being, and I will endeavour to use those terms when referring to a Sikh perspective.

There is also the legacy of colonialism to contend with; "Sikhism" as a term is arguably more a Western construct than anything else. Sikhs accept the term, because it is conventionally used, but might prefer to talk of Sikhi, understood as defining a worldview, an attitude, a way of life, not limited to simply religious practices in a place of worship(on this see Mandair 2013, 3-14). I will refer primarily to Sikhi in this book.

This chapter sets the scene, briefly discussing Guru Nanak as a pioneer of interfaith engagement and setting out core Sikh beliefs about the Guru Granth Sahib, as well as some key points of doctrine. Subsequent chapters discuss sections of the Guru Granth Sahib and also the *Janam Sakhis*, accounts of the life of Guru Nanak. Two further chapters explore previous dialogues and interfaith engagement between Christians and Sikhs. In the conclusion I offer some reflections on dialogue for today.

Guru Nanak and interfaith dialogue

Sikhi is a relatively young faith. Its founder, Guru Nanak, was born in 1469 CE not far from modern day Lahore, which is now part of Pakistan. The Guru travelled extensively, returning to Punjab in 1519 CE and establishing a settled community at Kartarpur where he lived for twenty years until his death in 1539. Harjot Oberoi notes that there were three phases to Guru Nanak's life: early contemplative; enlightenment experience with extensive travels; and a "foundational climax resulting in the establishment and gathering

INTRODUCTION

of the first Sikh community" (2000, 116). Oberoi explains Guru Nanak's conception of the divine as "eternal, infinite, all-pervasive; self-existent; and a perennial source of well-being, compassion, grace, and love." *Akal Purakh*, as Guru Nanak often termed the divine, is beyond time, the Creator, both possessing attributes and without attributes, formless and responding to the devotion of all worshippers, regardless of their caste or gender (2000, 118).

A series of nine successor Gurus led the developing community of Sikhs from 1539 to 1708, each contributing to the consolidation and institutionalisation of this faith. The tenth Guru, Gobind Singh, established the Guru Granth Sahib as the living Guru of the Sikh faith in the form of a sacred text. The focus of my exploration is primarily on Guru Nanak, his life, his writings and teachings, although I will discuss the other Gurus where relevant.

The Sikh faith has interfaith engagement at its core. Massey argues that Guru Nanak's whole life was characterised by interfaith dialogue. According to Massey, the Guru's focus was on understanding, not undermining the faith of others, and even his revelation that there is no Hindu or Muslim was to this end. Massey tells some well-known stories from the Guru's life, in which he urges the devout to a deeper and renewed piety. An example is found in Nanak's discussion with Daulat Khan on the real meaning of *namaz* (prayer), in which the Guru explains:

> Make mercy your mosque, faith your prayer-mat and righteousness your Quran.
>
> Make humility your circumcision, uprightness your fasting, and so you will be a (true) Muslim (AG 140).[1]

---

1. Following established convention, I will use AG to indicate a citation from the Adi Granth, or Guru Granth Sahib.

Guru Nanak and interfaith dialogue

Another example is a visit to Hardwar, where the Guru saw people throwing water at the sun to send it to their ancestors. Rather than rebuke them, he started throwing water towards his fields in Punjab. When the people questioned the efficacy of this action, the Guru's response was that if he could not throw water to his fields, why did they expect to throw water to their ancestors? The point the Guru was making was that religious ritual could all too easily become meaningless.

Finally, the tale of Guru Nanak's visit to Mecca is often told; he slept with his feet facing the Ka'aba, which was interpreted by the Muslims as a sign of disrespect. But, according to Sikh tradition, when they moved his body so his feet faced in a different direction, the Ka'aba also moved so Guru Nanak's feet were still facing it. When questioned on this, he replied that they were welcome to move his feet to face any direction where God was not. Since this was impossible, they left him alone. The Guru's teaching of the importance of true, active, faith over above religious ritual was emphasised again.

Massey's point is that Guru Nanak's aim was to challenge empty ritual and force people to think through the practice of their faith. He wanted to revive, not undermine, spiritual hunger and devotion (Massey 2010, 123-29). This chimes well with my own approach to interfaith engagement, which is greatly influenced by Stendhal's three rules for dialogue: to understand another religion, ask its adherents, not its enemies; don't compare your best with their worst; and leave space for "holy envy," that is, discovering aspects of the other religion which you admire (as cited in LeDonne and Behrendt 2017, xxv). This is the approach taken here.

INTRODUCTION

The Guru Granth Sahib within the Sikh faith

Cole argues that Sikhs are "a people of the book to an extent and in a manner which is not found in any other religion"(1982, 56), a view shared by other scholars. Guru Gobind Singh, the tenth Guru, brought some fundamental changes to the Sikh faith. He introduced the *Khalsa*, a word of Arabic origin that signifies purity, and refers to devout, initiated (*amritdhari*) Sikhs who have committed their lives to the practice of their faith. Members of the *Khalsa* are distinguished by their wearing the *panj kakke* (five Ks) of *kes* (uncut hair); *kangha* (a comb worn in the hair); *kirpan* (a sword); *kara* (a steel bangle) and *kachh* (cotton under-shorts).

Guru Gobind Singh also ended the line of human gurus, endowing the scripture, Sri Guru Granth Sahib, with the status of the Guru of all Sikhs. Oberoi explains that the Guru Granth Sahib is "not a work of genealogy, history or social code." Rather it is a collection of religious hymns, divided into three parts: "a brief introductory section made up of liturgical readings, a large middle portion, and an epilogue" (2000, 121). The middle portion of the text is organised around thirty-one *ragas* (Indian musical notations), which, Oberoi proposes, demonstrates that the text was gathered more for collective chanting and singing that for personal private reading. It is not just the text that is holy; the very language in which it is written is considered holy. The script used, which is called *Gurmukhi* (meaning "from the mouth of the Guru"), is believed to have been invented by the second Guru.

Jakobsh argues that the Guru Granth Sahib is unique amongst the scriptures of the religions of the world, as it is primarily hymns to be sung, not "a series of stories, parables or philosophical statements; nor is it a set of ethical precepts, arguments or a historical account" (2012, 3). Kaur Singh explains that Guru Gobind Singh did not pass his status as Guru to any of his disciples, but to the Guru Granth Sahib in perpetuity. "The Word alone was to be the Guru Eternal. The Guru Granth is thus revered as both the physical body of the Gurus and the metaphysical body of their poetry" (2011, 55). This is a unique understanding amongst the religions of the world. Whilst the Torah, the New Testament, the Vedas, the Qur'an are all important to adherents of those faiths, these are not the embodiment of Moses, the Apostles, the Rishis or the Prophet Muhammad. The Guru Granth Sahib has "the status of a juristic person," able to speak judgements as the living Guru of the Sikhs (Kaur Singh 2011, 57).

Mandair concurs that the Guru Granth Sahib is best described as a hymnal, adding that the modern standardised, 1430-page format was developed once the printing press was introduced into nineteenth century Punjab. He explains that the introductory section contains the *Japji* and Liturgical Sections and that the final section, which he terms an epilogue, contains miscellaneous texts and the *Raga Mala*. Within the main section of thirty-one *ragas*, the poems are organised from shortest to longest, beginning with the hymns of Guru Nanak and then those of the other Gurus in chronological order. They are distinguished using the codeword *Mohalla*, abbreviated to M. Thus, the hymns of Guru Nanak are labelled as M1 and so forth. Most *ragas* conclude with hymns by non-Sikh poets such as Kabir, Namdev and Farid. These authors are knowns as *bhagats*. The Guru Granth Sahib contains around six thousand compositions, of which 974 are attributed to Guru Nanak, 62 to Guru Angad, 907 to Guru Amar Das, 679 to Guru Ramdas, 2218 to Guru Arjan and 116 to Guru Tegh Bahadur. Kabir has the largest number of compositions of the *bhagats*, totalling 541. The key figure in the compilation of the text is undoubtedly Guru Arjan.

Mandair argues that music is central to the Guru Granth

INTRODUCTION

Sahib. As noted above, the text is arranged according to musical measures known as *ragas*. He explains

> A *raga* (along with the *tala* or rhythm) is a traditional melodic type in Hindustani music, consisting of a theme that expresses an aspect of spiritual feeling and sets forth a tonal system on which variations are improved within a prescribed framework of typical progressions, melodic formulas and rhythmic patterns (*talas*) (2013, 111).

The Gurus were skilled in contemporary Indian music; popular portraits of Guru Nanak show his constant companion Mardana to be a trained musician, playing the *rabab*, a stringed instrument. The compositions within the Guru Granth Sahib are therefore sung according to a particular style, so the emotion of the performance complements the meaning of the text (Mandair 2013, 109-12). Jakobsh concurs as to the primacy of music, explaining that the *rags* are believed to have eternal existence, to be discovered rather than designed or invented, reflecting the natural order and impacting the wellbeing of the universe. One *rag* might suggest joy, and thus be appropriate for a wedding, another is more suited to grieving, or to contemplation or celebrating the birth of a child. The sound of the *rags* together with the words of the Guru Granth Sahib are understood to purity the mind, leading to devotion and development of spiritual practice (2012, 4-5).

Oberoi explains that within Sikh theology, the main mode of revelation is the divine word, which is spoken aloud. Hence it is important not simply to silently read the Guru Granth Sahib, but for it to be vocalised and heard. This means that recitation of sacred texts is an integral part of a Sikh devotee's life. Guru Ram Das, the fourth Guru, prescribed a routine for the believer, which is cited below:

The Guru Granth Sahib within the Sikh faith

> He who calls himself a Sikh of the true Guru, he should get up in the early hours of the morning and recite the Name of God. He should make effort to rise before dawn and take a bath. By repeating the Lord's Name, under the guidance of the Guru, all his troubles will end and all his blemishes be destroyed. Then when the day dawns, he should sing the *bani* of the Guru and remember the name of the Supreme Being while sitting or moving. He who remembers my Lord with every breath and loaf, that Gursikh is dear to the Guru. He on whom my Lord showers His Blessings, the Guru instructs that Gursikh. I beg for the dust of the feet of that Gursikh, who not only recites the Word of God but also makes others repeat it. (AG 305-6, as translated in Oberoi 2000, 125).

Thus, both memorisation and recitation of the divine word are integral to Sikh identity. Mastering the text is therefore necessary for practise of the faith, and so children are expected to learn at least a few basic texts by heart in order to be able to participate in the worshipping life of the community.

Oberoi argues that there are three congregational activities within a gurdwara that centre on the sacred text. First, the daily devotion; bringing out the Guru Granth Sahib each morning, laying the Guru on a specially constructed lectern with canopy. The Guru is opened and read from, always attended by a *granthi*, an official reader, and remains open all day for devotees to pay their respects; at the end of the day, the Guru Granth Sahib is transported with solemnity to a resting place within the shrine for the night.

The second activity is *sangat* (congregational) worship, which consists of singing hymns from the scripture. This is often *kirtan*, congregational singing, normally led by *ragis*, professional singers. *Ragis* are often extensively trained and can command significant followings; recordings of their singing are played in Sikh homes. Third, the *granthi* will discourse on the text of the Guru Granth Sahib during the day (2000, 126-27).

The Guru Granth Sahib is also important for personal piety. Oberoi explains that devout Sikhs begin each day by taking the *hukam* (commandment) or *vak* (reciting God's word). The text is placed on a lectern and opened at random. The devotee recites the first hymn at the top of the left-hand page, and this becomes the *hukam* for that day. The devotee meditates on its meaning throughout that day. This ritual is carried out both at home by devout Sikhs and also in every gurdwara, with the *hukam* of the day often shared online (2000, 128).

Within the early Sikh community, two doctrines were held. First, the teaching of Guru-Panth, that the community was supreme and that all were equal within the community. Second, the teaching of Guru-Granth, that the Scripture was supreme. Oberoi argues that this tension only became problematic when Sikhs attained military and political power. If all were equal, he asks, how could a Sikh kingdom be ruled? In response to this challenge, Maharaja Ranjit Singh emphasised the supremacy and importance of Scripture over above the Panth, a trend that continued after the Sikh empire was conquered by the British. The reform movement, Singh Sabha, which developed as the British Empire took power in Punjab, also emphasised the Guru Granth Sahib, primarily, Oberoi proposes, as a fixed point in an otherwise shifting and confusing world. This led eventually to a more uniform and structured approach to the interpretation of the sacred text (2000, 129).

The Guru Granth Sahib plays a prominent role in life cycle rituals. Soon after a child is born, she or he is given *am-*

The Guru Granth Sahib within the Sikh faith

rit, sacred nectar, to drink, and a recitation from the Scripture is made, including the prologue and the first five stanzas of *Japji*, the opening composition of the Guru Granth Sahib. Within a few days of being born, the child is taken to the gurdwara for a naming ceremony. The Guru Granth Sahib is opened at random; the child is given a name which will have the same letter as the first composition on the left-hand page.

If a child, or an adult, wishes to be admitted into the Khalsa, then the initiation ceremony, *amrit sanskar*, is performed in the presence of the Guru Granth Sahib and at least five Sikhs who have already been initiated. These five recite from set portions of the text: *Japji, Jap*, the ten *Savvayyas, Benati Chaupai* and the six prescribed stanzas from *Anand Sahib*. At the end of the ceremony, a *hukam* is also taken.

When Sikhs get married, the bride and groom circumambulate the Guru Granth Sahib four times. While they do this, those leading the ceremony, often three *ragis*, sing set hymns from the Guru Granth Sahib. When a Sikh dies, before the cremation, the Guru Granth Sahib is read continuously, either by members of the family or by professional readers. After the cremation, the family initiates a complete reading of the whole of the Guru Granth Sahib, either at home or in a gurdwara (Oberoi 2000, 130-31). It is therefore clear that the Guru Granth Sahib is at the centre of a Sikh's life; even those who are more nominal in their practice of their faith will nevertheless regularly engage with their Guru as they go through different stages in life.

I will close this section with a story that illustrates the way in which the Guru Granth Sahib functions as the Guru for Sikhs. Cole recounts how in 1920 a significant number of Punjabis of low caste status sought to improve their situation either through converting to Christianity or by taking initiation into the Khalsa Panth. Some, who remembered that the first Gurus had opposed caste discrimination, welcomed

INTRODUCTION

those who had taken initiation. But not all were so disposed. For those conscious of caste status and pollution, the problem was that by eating with those of low social status, they themselves would be considered polluted, and thus unable to eat with their contemporaries who had high status.[2]

This issue had to be resolved. It was brought to a head after a mass *amrit* ceremony in Amritsar, when those who had taken initiation wished to make pilgrimage to *Harmandir Sahib*, also referred to as the Golden Temple. A dispute arose as to the appropriate course of action; it looked unresolvable at first, but then it was agreed to consult the Guru Granth Sahib. The text was opened at random and these words were read:

> Upon the worthless he bestows his grace, brother, if they will serve the True Guru. Exalted is the service of the True Guru, brother, to hold in remembrance the divine name. God himself offers grace and mystic union. We are meritless transgressors, brother, yet the True Guru has drawn us to that blissful union. (AG 638 as cited in Cole 1982, 65).

It became clear to all that those described as "worthless" and "meritless transgressors" were those of low caste status. It was therefore clear that they should be welcomed into the community and be treated as equal members (Cole 1982, 64-65).

2. The issue of caste and Sikhi is a complex one. Jakobsh observes that although caste was rejected by the Gurus because of a belief that all were equal before *Waheguru*, in practice discrimination based on caste status still exists in the present day, in that Sikhs tend to relate most closely with those of their own caste. She concludes that "the Sikh Gurus thus opposed the spiritual ramifications of caste but accepted caste as a form of social organization fundamental to the society in which they lived" (2012, 80-81). Jaspal and Takhar (2016) indicate that caste remains an issue for British Sikhs.

Some key teachings within Sikhi

In this section, I set out some core teachings of Sikhi, as explored in Shackle and Mandair's reader *Teachings of the Sikh Gurus*. Amongst other topics, they explore impermanence; mind, self and ego; action and grace; and Guru as work. Each of these four areas are discussed below.

Impermanence

Guru Nanak's teaching follows a classic style of metaphor in Indian poetry, equating a human being's life with a single night, describing the passing of the night in terms of infancy, childhood, youth and old age. The aim is to remind the hearer that death is inevitable and cannot be avoided. Time is described as a paradox, neither real nor illusory, but also both; neither subjective nor objective, but also both; time is the matrix in which we are trapped, but also a gift. Ultimately time is both a gift and a curse.

Birth takes many forms, not necessarily just human, and birth into different human circumstances, all of which require relationship with the Guru above all else. This means that relationships are just for this present life. Once the eternal self, the *jiva,* is reborn in a different body, the relationships and memories of a previous existence cease. The pleasures of life are fleeting; we chase after them, but in reality, they have no permanence. Shackle and Mandair quote from AG 536:

> In this world love is false, I see,
> All chase their own delight, both spouse and friend.
> "You're mine", all say to those they think they love,

INTRODUCTION

> It's strange these ties are broken in the end.
> This stupid mind still does not get my point –
> The world-sea's only crossed by praising God.
>   (2005, 28).

Death comes all too soon; we may think we are immortal, but we really are not. This means we should take advantage of what little time we have in order to prepare ourselves for what is to come, engaging in spiritual disciplines and recognising that spiritual growth only happens if we put in enough effort. Moreover, relationship with the divine is all that really matters. Whether it is the challenges and problems of life, or whether it is being in a time of plenty and provision, if one does not have a clear relationship with *Akal Purakh*, what is the point of it all? (Shackle and Mandair 2005, 24-31).

Mandair adds that the core message that Guru Nanak taught was that in order to experience Oneness through unity with the divine one must recognise and acknowledge *hukam*, the law of impermanence. Time is both subjective and objective, a teaching that, as noted above, is expressed through collapsing a human life into a single night, which consists of four watches:

> A momentary guest, man comes into this world to sort things out.
> But the fool is trapped by worldly greed
> Till, seized by death, he repents when he departs.
>
> The reaper, when he comes, cuts both ripe and unripe,
> He makes his preparations, picking up his scythe,
> For once the farmer orders, the crop is cut and weighed.

> The first watch is wasted on busyness, the next in sleep,
> The third in idle talk, and in the fourth dawn breaks,
> The One from which life springs is never once remembered.

The Guru teaches that one is born mortal, knowing one with die; the dawn is coming, but this is not something to celebrate, but rather something to recognise as an illusion. It is in the night, when dreaming, that we have a clearer experience of reality (Mandair 2013, 141).

Mind, Self, Ego

Mind is understood in two senses. First, as mind-as-ego, the aspect of a person which exists under the influence of self-centredness (*haumai*). This mind-as-ego is aware of both self and that which exists externally, but is sadly crippled by spiritual sickness. The mind is responsible for plotting, desires, anger, negative emotions, "away from its true home or natural state, and consequently subject to continual coming and going through different life-forms" (Shackle and Mandair 2005, 41).

Second, if this mind renounces ego and instead orientates around the Guru's word, then it becomes the "beloved mind." Within Sikh teaching, liberation is not achieved through austerity and discipline or annihilation of the ego. Rather it comes through defeat of the five enemies of lust, anger, greed, attachment and ego, together with appropriate recognition of one's inter-connection with the rest of creation.

In the texts that Shackle and Mandair have selected, it is clear that release for the mind comes through taking refuge

INTRODUCTION

in the Lord, concentrating on the divine Name above all else. If the mind seeks pleasure, this simply results in pain and separation; far better to devote oneself to the divine. The Guru is the only one who can truly enable the mind to be free of its own passions and desires, which blind the self to one's own sickness. The image of the mind as "an elephant raging in rut" is a powerful one of a deeply destructive force, which also has the potential to create, if only it can be harnessed and channelled properly.

Within the Sikh understanding it is clear that all of the created order is sick and suffering, a term referred to as *dukh*. The point is made clear in the refrain of the fourth text Shackle and Mandair quote:

> The sicknesses of ego make
> A single pain, seen everywhere.
> Relief's appointed through the Word (2005, 44).

The point is that the human ego and desire for mastery cause untold pain and suffering. The text goes on to list all those who are sick, with the delusion of control and the overwhelm caused by personal desire. It is only through the Guru's Word that release can be obtained. It makes me think of Paul's opening statements in his letter to the Romans, about how all have sinned and fallen short of the glory of God; that there is no one who does good, all are destined for destruction, but it is only through the grace of God as revealed in Jesus that we can be saved.

The other texts reinforce this same teaching. Another sets out the view that all we do, say and think is done in and conditioned by our ego. A different text sets out how ego is both the problem and the source of the solution; ego is a chronic illness which contains its own cure. But how many actually find that cure?

Some key teachings within Sikhi

The ego cannot be controlled through austerities; there is no point in going into the desert to meditate or in trying to quell one's mind by force. What is needed is the Guru; his Name and the divine are what stills the mind. The ego and the divine Name are mutually exclusive; where one is present, the other cannot be. The problem comes where the "five enemies" are given space to take territory within a person. Shackle and Mandair cite Guru Granth Sahib 1358, which deals with each "enemy" in turn. Attachment is the most powerful, bewitching even the strongest; lust steals thoughts, giving brief pleasure that soon dissipates into destitution and pain; anger makes people dance like monkeys, controlling the sinful; greed causes people to race to-and-fro, desperately seeking things that do not last; and ego wearies us with endless life and death, trapping people in the cycle of rebirth (2005, 49-50).

Mandair concurs that Guru Nanak's teaching of *hukam*, impermanence, illustrates the fundamental human problem. We become attached to that which will not last, including our own egos, and in the process, we lose contact with the divine, which is the source of all. Nanak therefore speaks to his own mind – hence the repeated refrain of "O Nanak" at the end of his compositions – as his unconscious mind calls to his conscious mind to join together in unity (2013, 143-44).

Jakobsh adds that within Sikh thought, human beings have an innate connection with *Akal Purakh*, the Creator, and that Guru Nanak taught that the human soul emanates from the light of *Waheguru*. This means human beings are born essentially good. But the problem is that of *haumai*, "reliance on the self in the absence of a recognition of one's ultimate dependence on God." At the same time, human beings are *manmukh*, "bound to the ego and centred on the self" (2012, 49).[3]

---

3. The term *man* is particularly hard to translate. It is often rendered as "ego" or "self," but can also indicate the "heart" as in the site of thought and of feelings (Kaur Singh 1995, 60).

INTRODUCTION

Ethical Being: Action and Grace

Shackle and Mandair begin their discussion by explaining:

> Once the nature of ego and time are understood to be intrinsically linked, a rather more interesting and complex picture of ethical action emerges from the hymns of the Sikh Gurus than the stereotypical opposition between a passive karma and an active notion of divine grace (2005, 75).

Shackle and Mandair add that within the Sikh worldview, karma is inherent in the nature of existence. Existence itself is explained as "a writing (*lekh*) that is held in place by a fabric made of space, time and cause" (2005, 75). This means that the divine is understood as a continually flowing action. Hence any action committed by an ego, by an individual self, which is by definition distinct from the One, acts against that flow of divine writing, "effectively creating eddies that attempt to freeze the flux of existence" (2005, 76). These eddies endure; hence all egotistical action has longer lasting consequences, as karma builds up, separating the ego from the divine.

Karma is explained through reference to the law of conservation of energy, albeit applied to thoughts, speech, desires and feelings. One's rebirth is therefore a consequence of one's own actions. As Shackle and Mandair put it, an action "is like a seed which must bear fruit either in this life or the next" (2005, 76). Actions can all too easily develop into habits, which can even be carried into a subsequent life if one does not perform appropriate meritorious actions to counteract the impact of ill-considered choices.

The way to deal with this problem is to become *gurmukh* (literally Guru-facing), that is, turned towards the Guru, no longer acting on the basis of one's ego. Those who are still bound by ego are called *manmukh* (literally self-facing), that is, self-centred. Those who remain under the control of the ego (*haumai*) are condemned to being continually reborn in ignorance, unable to escape the sickness of their ego. It is only through divine grace that one is freed from this cycle, and so able to enter into the free existence of the one who is centred only on obedience to the divine.

Kaur Singh translates *haumai* as "I-Myself," and describes the problem as the individual "constantly centering on 'I', 'me' and 'mine', the self is circumscribed as a particular person, wrenched from his/her universal root." Building on the selfish ego, an individual becomes separated from the One Reality, and the divine spark is veiled as the selfish person becomes *manmukh*(turned towards me) rather than *gurmukh* (turned towards the Guru) (2011, 71).

Mandair argues that the Punjabi word for karma, *karam,* has three meanings. First, to accomplish, do, cause. Second, when linked with *avagavan* (coming and going, the cycle of birth and death) it indicates fate, destiny, transmigration. Third, it is "conceptually synonymous with the terms *nadar* and *kirpa* (implying grace) and the Persian term *hukam* (order/command/will/call, etc.)" (2013, 145). He distinguishes the Sikh and Vedic understandings of karma, arguing that the Sikh concept concentrates on the ideas associated with the third meaning given above. The focus of the Gurus' teaching is on *karam,* defined as actions in accordance with, or working against, *hukam*. As noted above, those who work against *hukam* are working against the writing (*lekh*) of the universe, and so leave traces within the fabric of reality, which prolong the separation of the ego from the divine (2013, 144-46).

INTRODUCTION

Guru as Word

Shackle and Mandair explain that within Sikh doctrine, whilst the generic term Guru indicates a teacher of spiritual insights or worldly knowledge, it has deeper meanings as well. It refers to Guru Nanak and his successors, as well as to the divine light that is manifested in all ten Gurus and the authority vested in the name "Nanak." Before the death of the tenth Nanak, Guru Gobind Singh, spiritual authority was conferred on the Adi Granth in 1708 CE, henceforth the Guru Granth Sahib. This is the doctrine of scripture or Word as Guru (*shabad-guru*) (2005, 103).

Guru Nanak explains that his own guru is the Word; he denies that he can speak of anything himself. By renouncing his own ego and status, Guru Nanak vests himself with the authority of that which he has heard. Shackle and Mandair argue there are resonances in his position with the doctrine of *anhad shabad*, the "unspoken Word," that is, the Word that speaks into the mind since "the mind is the true mint in which the formless divine is configured as Word"(2005, 104). This means that the communication is not so much between self and another as it is of the mind with itself.

The expectation is therefore not of external revelation but rather of the mind becoming a receptacle for the Name, which is the purest of all words. In the hymns that Shackle and Mandair cite, there is a fluid interchange between Word(*shabad*), Guru, and Name (*nam*), "all of which are synonymous with the ultimate authority in Sikhism, which is defined as the site where ego is lacking" (2005, 105).

This is a really good example of how different religions use the same word to mean similar but in fact radically different things. There is a complex discussion to be had about how "the Name" is used within Judaism to refer to God, how "the Word" was the creative principle within neo-Platonic

Some key teachings within Sikhi

philosophy, which was then co-opted by Philo within Judaism and by John within Christianity, each using the term to mean slightly different things. Here in Sikhi, we have the same words, but a vastly different meaning. Beware in dialogue of talking at cross purposes because you have not adequately defined your terms. An easy way to illustrate this point is this text:

> With no faith in the guru, with no love for the Word,
> Even hundreds of births cannot ever bring peace.
> Nanak, the gurmukh is easily joined through his love with the Real.
> (AG 591, cited in Shackle and Mandair 2005, 109).

There are other texts that could also be used to emphasise the point, but this is sufficient for the moment. The main point is simply that within Sikhi, the Word is the one who prevents rebirth as the mind is healed of its own sickness of *haumai* (ego) and becomes instead free to be fully absorbed in the bliss of relating to the divine. This is very different from the way the Word is described in John 1:1-5.

As Mandair explains, Guru Nanak taught that he himself did not speak; it was the Word that spoke; hence the teaching of *anhad shabad*, the "unspoken Word."

> As *anhad shabad* the Word itself speaks or resounds without being spoken. This sounds like a tautology but actually indicates a mode of communication in which ego no longer controls the production of words, nor indeed the process of making words into things. Removed from the grasp of ego, words are no longer given

> value according to their degree of correspondence to things, but instead arise from an internalized mode of speech that occurs between consciousness (ego) and unconscious (non-ego) mind (2013, 152).

The Word is therefore spoken from the unconscious mind to enlighten the conscious mind and enable realization of true identity and so union with the divine.

This chapter has offered a brief overview of a few core concepts within Sikhi. It has done little more than scratch the surface, but this does serve as an orientation and outline for the chapters that follow. There are, broadly speaking, three distinct foci: first on the opening sections of the Guru Granth Sahib; second on the stories of Guru Nanak's life, contrasted primarily with the accounts of Jesus' life found in the Gospels; and third examples of dialogue between Christians and Sikhs.

Chapter 2

A Christian's thoughts about *Mul Mantar*

I have often found discussion of sacred texts to be a useful route into interfaith dialogue; it can be difficult to know where to begin the conversation, and having an objective, fixed text, or texts, in front of you is one straightforward way of beginning talking together. That is my aim in this chapter, although of course this is not strictly speaking a dialogue or a conversation, as I am not actually talking with anyone else. Rather I have read the *mul mantar*, read what others say about it, and then reflected from my own Christian perspective on what I have understood from my reading. Doubtless I have got some things wrong, and doubtless other things could be said. But my aim is not to be definitive; it is to think and learn. In what follows, I introduce the *mul mantar*, and then examine it phrase by phrase, first through the writings of scholars of the Sikh faith, especially Kaur Singh (1995) and Massey (2010), and second through my own reflections on the understanding I have developed through reading the text and the exposition of others.

Reading the Mul Mantar

The opening verses of the Guru Granth Sahib are widely agreed to constitute a succinct summary of the teachings of Guru Nanak. As Christopher Shackle explains:

> But the single greatest composition by Guru Nanak is unquestionably his great *Japji*, which is designed for individual meditative recitation as the first item of the daily discipline of observance and which is accordingly placed at the very beginning of the Scripture (AG:1-8). Unlike most of the poems in the Adi Granth, which are each written in a single metre throughout, the *Japji* is an extraordinarily original composition made up of thirty-eight main stanzas, which are notably varied in metre while also being connected into larger units through repetitions and refrains (2016, 112).

Michael Shapiro goes even further, proposing that

> It is commonly stated within Sikh tradition that in a sense the entire contents of the Guru Granth Sahib is encapsulated in the *Japji*, which in turn is encapsulated by the *mul mantar* that stands at the very beginning of *Japji*, which is even further epitomized in the *ikomkar* with which the *mul mantar* commences (2016, 218).

The opinion of these two non-Sikh scholars, which is also shared by Sikhs, imply that a detailed study of the opening of Guru Granth Sahib is the best place to begin if one wishes to understand Sikh thought. In what follows I will explore the *mul mantar* in detail, engaging with scholarly explanations of the text and discussing my own Christian responses to what is being taught. This study is limited in that it engages with English translations of the text, and as the discussion below will illustrate, much is lost in translation, or even in transliteration.

The *mul mantar* can be transcribed as follows:

> *Ik omkar, satnam, karta purakh, nirbhau, nirvair, akal murat, ajuni, saibhang, gurprasad.*

There is so much to consider in this brief statement of the core beliefs of Sikhi and in what follows each phrase will be discussed in turn. But first three representative translations of the whole text:

James Massey's translation of the *mul mantar* is as follows:

> He is Sole Supreme Being; eternal manifestation;
> Creator, immanent Reality; Without Fear;
> Without Rancour; timeless Form; Unincarnated;
> Self-existent; Realized by grace of the holy Preceptor (2010, 19)

Shackle and Mandair offer a slightly different translation:

> One God/Reality Exists, Whose Name is True,
> Creative Power, Without Fear, Without Enmity,
> Timeless Form, Unborn, Self-Existent, By the
> Guru's grace (2005, xxvi-xxvii).

Kaur Singh translates using more gender inclusive language than Massey:

A CHRISTIAN'S THOUGHTS ABOUT *MUL MANTAR*

> There is One Being
> Truth by Name
> Primal Creator
> Without fear
> Without enmity
> Timeless in form
> Unborn
> Self-existent
> The grace of the Guru (1995, 51)

In the introduction to her translation, Kaur Singh explains that many religious terms carry with them implicit Jewish or Christian meanings, giving as an example the word "soul," which she says indicates a "bipartite framework, one in which the body is not only subordinated to the soul but also given a negative identity" (1995, 40). This is certainly true of Platonic thought, although whether it also applies to the biblical conception of personhood is a moot point. But even if there is a Christian understanding of soul and body being one, it is different from the Sikh framework which presumes "there is one light and the light is also the body (AG 125), and that the primary distinction is between "the *self* cognizant of its essence versus the *self* ignorantly turned towards its ego" (1995, 40). Kaur Singh writes elsewhere about the importance of fresh translations which pay attention to patriarchal and gender-specific assumptions that are a distortion of the Sikh understanding of the divine (2011, 117-18). For the purposes of my discussion, I will refer to her translations to illustrate the need to be aware of unnecessarily gendered language that import meanings which are not present in the original.

Even a cursory glance at the three translations above indicates the points of particular controversy and challenge for the translator. Arguably the hardest phrase of all to translate is the first, *ik omkar*.

Ik omkar

Massey concurs with Shapiro that *ik omkar* has a unique place in Sikhi as the essence of the *mul mantar*, which is itself the essence of Sikhi.[1] He points out that in the Guru Granth Sahib, *ik* is the numeral 1, not the word One, before adding that the phrase is almost impossible to translate. He lists seven English attempts to illustrate his point. They are:

- There is but one God
- ... The One Supreme Being ...
- He is the Sole Supreme Being
- The One Universal Being
- He is One. He is the First. He is all that is
- God is One and all-pervading
- There is one Supreme Being

Massey then explores the views of Bhai Gurdas, scribe of the first copy of the Adi Granth, and the Uncle of Guru Arjan, who lived during the lifetime of four Sikh Gurus and helped Guru Arjan with the compilation of the Adi Granth. Discussing the meaning of *ik omkar*, Bhai Gurdas explains: "After taking form, the Formless became One. From One originates the syllable-sound, which has the form of *Omkar*."

The succession of events is first that the formless one (the divine) takes form, and that form becomes the syllable-sound of *Omkar*, which is behind the entire visible universe. Another early commentator, Gyani Badan Singh, wrote his commentary in response to the translation of the Adi Granth

---

1. I am following Massey's transliteration here. Others would argue for *ik onkar* or *ik oankar* as better transliterations.

A CHRISTIAN'S THOUGHTS ABOUT *MUL MANTAR*

by Ernest Trumpp. Gyani Badan Singh's position is Vedantic; he argues for the non-dual nature of reality, and equates *ik omkar* with the Hindu sacred sound of *om*. He goes so far as to argue that the figure 1 at the start of the text is "a veil before *Omkar*, so that persons belonging to a low caste and women may also use it in their devotion," because women and those of low caste were not allowed to utter the sacred sound *om* (Massey 1991, 30). A third interpreter, Sahib Singh, also focuses on *om*. He argues for three uses of *om*: first, as a sacred symbol at the beginning and end of the Vedas and other religious books; second, to answer a question, as a sign of respect; and third, *Om* as Brahman. Sahib Singh adds that 1 is a prefix that puts stress on these meanings, and *kar* is a Sanskrit suffix, used with nouns to indicate "One unchangeable essence." Thus *ik omkar* indicates the one timeless Being who is all-pervading in one essence (Massey 1991, 24-30).

Massey gives further examples of Nanak's own views on *ik omkar*. For example, Guru Nanak writes "My Lord is One, He is One, He is One, brother," stressing the unity and singularity of the divine. Massey explains that this phrase is the opening of a longer hymn, which begins with an expectation of meditation on the Oneness of God. In another, longer, section of a different hymn, Guru Nanak writes

> On the first day, One Absolute Being – unique, eternal, unincarnated, without identity, without impurity, inaccessible, imperceptible, without form or outline; but through an ongoing search, (I have) seen (Him) in each and every heart.

Here Guru Nanak sets out the absolute nature of the unity of God and his all-pervading nature. Guru Nanak's writing is full of references to God as One, including descriptions of One Giver, One Essence, ages to ages One Form, True Lord

Ik omkar

One, One Absolute Lord, One Teacher, you One Creator, One Soul, One King. These are but a few examples of many, which serve to illustrate the point that for Guru Nanak in particular, and Sikhs in general, the absolute unity of God is foundational to their faith (Massey 1991, 33-36).

Guru Nanak also used negative definition to indicate his point about monotheism, relying repeatedly on the phrase "no one else at all." For example, in one hymn, he writes "No one else is seen, whom I should praise, no one else is there to equal Him" and elsewhere "The light of the Supreme Lord fills the three worlds, No-one else except him is there, O brother" (Massey 1991, 36-37). Guru Nanak makes repeated reference to the divine as Creator, Source and Origin of all that exists, for example stating, "From One Lamp was lit (another) lamp, in this way he has shown (the pervading) Light of the three worlds." Massey explains that the true Guru, God, is himself the Light that is already burning. It is through this Light that others see the light which pervades the three worlds; thus the One Creator is an all-pervading presence throughout everything which exists. For Guru Nanak, *Akal Purakh* is both Source and Presence of everything. Finally, Massey draws attention to Guru Nanak's phrase "He is I and I am He," which indicates that the human self and the One or Creator Lord are non-different, as the Divine is permanently present within each and every human heart (1991, 37-40).

Massey suggests that referring to "One God" is an indication of the influence of Christian and Semitic concepts, and that renderings such as "One Supreme Being," "Sole Supreme Being," or "the One Universal Being" are closer to Nanak's thought (1991, 47). Massey concludes:

> The figure "1" preceding Omkaru cannot possibly be replaced with the word "one," because it includes all the shades of the meanings contained in various expressions used by Nanak like

> *eko* (repeated) ("only one"), *ekamkaru* ("One Absolute Being"), *avaru na duja* ("no one else at all," or literally, "no one else second"), *eka mahi saraba* ("One in all") and *nirala* ("unique"). The position of the figure "1" should be considered as emphatic, communicating the idea of "Absolute" or "Ultimate." So the possible rendering of figure "1" or "Ik" here can be "One Absolute…" (1991, 51-52).

Pashaura Singh concurs with Massey's assessment, arguing that by beginning with the numeral 1, the Guru Granth Sahib emphasises the singularity of the divine. *Omkar* is described at length in Guru Nanak's composition *Ramakali Dakkhani*. Here he explains that *Omkar* fashioned consciousness, and is the source of mountains, ages, the Vedas, all things. By the grace of *Omkar* people were liberated through the teachings of the Guru. The transforming power of *Omkar* provides the means of achieving awareness of higher realities, and is the foundational Word (*shabad*), which is "the basis of the whole creation of time and space and represents in seed form all scriptural revelation" (Pashaura Singh 2016, 227). Pashaura Singh summarises his understanding of the divine as both male and female, as creator and sustainer:

> As the creator and sustainer of the universe, Akal Purakh lovingly watches over it. As a father figure he runs the world with justice, and destroys evil and supports good. As a mother figure, the Supreme Being is the source of love and grace, and responds to the devotion of her humblest followers (2016, 228).

Nikky-Guninder Kaur Singh translates the phrase she transliterates as *Ikk Oan Kar* as "one being is." She elaborates:

Ik omkar

> Here, three modes of knowledge have been used to signify the Divine – numerical, alphabetical and geometrical. The prime number '1' is recognized by people of every language and culture. It is followed by the alpha of the Gurmukhi script, also a sign for *Oan* ('being'; Sanskrit *Aum*). It is completed by the sign for *Kar* (Is), a geometrical arc reaching away into space. While the former two constitute the beginning of the mathematical and verbal languages, the arc is without beginning or end. The existence of the One gestures motion and movement – an opening to countless possibilities (2011, 59).

The point about the unity of the Divine being stressed numerically, alphabetically and geometrically is an important one; the living Guru speaks of the identity of *Waheguru* beyond merely using words. Kaur Singh discusses conceptions of monotheism, arguing that the Sikh understanding finds no incompatibility between unity and plurality, citing a text of the Guru Granth Sahib which states, "from the One issue myriads and into the One they are ultimately assimilated"(AG 131). The point is that Sikh monotheism is inclusivist, believing all share the same Divine sovereign, the One True Being (2011, 61).

Kaur Singh warns of the dangers of translation, especially of the risk that *Ikk Oan Kar* might be inadvertently constrained if it is rendered "There is One God," for the phrase "does not quite express the vastness, the plenitude or the intimacy bursting forth in the original." Her concern is that "God" is invariably conceived as male, interpreted within Judaeo-Christian patriarchal assumptions, limiting our conception of the divine and harming our relationships with our fellow human beings. As an alternative, Kaur Singh cites Mary Daly's suggestion of "Be-ing" as closer to the Guru's intention and meaning (2011, 65). Kaur Singh quotes the Guru

Granth Sahib, including the identification of the divine as both male and female (AG 1020) and Guru Arjan's exclamation of the divine: "You are my father, you are my mother, you are my brother, you are my friend" (AG 103). Kaur Singh also discusses the metaphor of a Sikh's attachment to the divine being contrasted with a mother's milk for a child, illustrated by the statement, "my mind loves the Divine, O my life, like a child loves suckling milk" (AG 538) (2011, 104-6).

There is nothing here that a Christian can disagree with, except, for some, the idea of love and grace indicating a mother, rather than a father figure. But is it not imperative on Christians to recognise that the divine is beyond a binary ascription of human gender? Arguably conversation with Sikhs can help Christians rids themselves of patriarchal baggage as they develop a more holistic understanding of the God whom they worship.

My reflections

God is One, but what is meant by that phrase varies from faith to faith. It is surprising how many different understandings of the unity of the divine exist within the world religions. At the very least, five different world faiths all subscribe to a form of monotheism, but understand this term differently. It would be a distraction to elaborate in great detail, but brief, oversimplified, summaries are potentially useful for the discussion. Within Judaism, God is one and has no partner or form. Yet as Judaism has developed over time, divine attributes (wisdom, for example) are identified as distinct. The divine name is revealed to Moses, but becomes so sacred it can only be addressed by circumlocution. Thus, epithets such as "the Most High" or "the Name" are used, including when reading the text of the Hebrew Bible.

Within Islam, God is addressed, in Arabic, as Allah. The Arabic language has a particular resonance for Islam, as the

Ik omkar

Quran is believed to be complete and inspired only in its original form. Some more theologically conservative Muslims argue that Allah indicates the Islamic God. Linguists point out that Arabic speaking Christians use Allah in their worship as well. But this point does not deter Muslims who presume to say Allah is to indicate the God of Islam. Allah is understood as unapproachable, transcendent, majestic and sovereign, determining the fate of all human beings. Allah is closer to a human than his jugular vein (Quran 50:16), yet at the same time he remains aloof. He is described in terms of *tawhid*, the unity or oneness of God, as in the *shahada,* the Islamic declaration of faith: "There is no god but God [Allah]."

Within *sanatan dharma*, as Hindus prefer their belief and worldview to be termed, there are a wide range of views about the divine. It is common for Hindus who reside in the United Kingdom to describe themselves as monotheists, primarily through an analogy of a prism. Just as white light is split into an infinite rainbow of colours by a prism, so the argument goes, so the pantheon of Hindu deities in fact displays the rainbow of divine diversity, behind which lies the singular unity of Brahmin. For other Hindus, a particular manifestation (avatar) of the divine is the supreme Lord; the Hare Krishna belief in Krishna fulfilling this role is probably the clearest and best-known example. A Hare Krishna described his belief to me as "polymorphic monotheism," that is to say, belief in one God who manifests in different forms at different times and circumstances for different reasons.

Sikhs also argue that *Waheguru*, the divine, is one. *Waheguru* is above gender, encompassing both male and female, above ethnicity, class, caste and any other division or marker that humanity have chosen to impose upon themselves. While Christians might want to argue for an equivalence of their own beliefs, this would be mistaken. A Sikh can talk comfortably about God as Father and Mother in a way most Christians would not. This is not always reflected in English translations of the Guru Granth Sahib; as the discussion above illustrates, the feminist translations of Nikky Guninder Kaur Singh highlight the unthinking patriarchal assumptions of some (Western) interpreters of the Guru Granth Sahib.

The fact that Jesus Christ is a man is also relevant here; while the Sikh Gurus are also men, they do not have the same status in their faith as Jesus does in Christianity. Perhaps the closest Christian doctrine to the Sikh belief is Irenaeus' theory of recapitulation, which is most neatly summarised in his statement that "what is not assumed is not healed." By this Irenaeus meant that Jesus Christ was fully human, entering into and experiencing the full limitations and frustrations of human existence. But he remained without sin or failure. Feminist theologians would, perhaps, point out that Jesus becoming a man potentially excludes women, but the traditional response is that there is universality in particularity. That is to say, by becoming a specific human being, Jesus therefore represents all humanity. As St Paul explains to the believers in Galatia, "there is no longer Jew nor Gentile, there is no longer slave nor free, there is no longer male and female; for all of you are one in Christ Jesus (Galatians 3:28, NRSV). Both Christians and Sikhs (not to mention Jews, Muslims, Hindus and many others) believe that God is one, but what we mean by that statement will vary from person to person, within and between our respective faiths.

Manifest as Word

Some would separate out *omkar* as a distinct phrase and translate it as "manifest as Word." What Christian can hear those words, and not immediately hear this resonance?

> In the beginning was the Word, and the Word was with God, and the Word was God. He was

> in the beginning with God. All things came into being through him, and without him not one thing came into being. What has come into being in him was life, and the life was the light of all people. The light shines in the darkness, and the darkness did not overcome it.(John 1:1-5, NRSV).

Yet resonances are not identity, and as the discussion of "one" above indicates, the same word may have completely different meanings depending on the context within which it is spoken. The opening verses of John's Gospel are a position statement, claiming a particular theological position vis-a-vis the Judaism and Greek philosophy of the time. The Word, the *logos* in the Greek of the day, was understood as the divine creative principle. John's Gospel argues that this Word must be identified with a particular human being, Jesus of Nazareth. The whole text can be understood as establishing and defending this theological position.

For Sikhs, the Guru Granth Sahib is a written text but also a living Guru, a person not a book. The Word that is manifest is written, yet alive. The Guru Granth Sahib speaks daily to the faithful, and must be revered and treated as the manifestation of a Guru. While Christians speak of their Bible as the Word of God, they do not treat the written text with anything like the veneration afforded to the Guru Granth Sahib, which is understood to be a living Guru. The difference is illustrated by the growing emphasis amongst Sikhs on referring to the "pages" of the Guru Granth Sahib as "angs," that is, as "limbs."

Conservative evangelical Christians, arguably amongst the most committed to the inerrancy and efficacy of the written word, are perfectly happy to write notes in the margins of their Bibles, or highlight particular passages. There is even a popular cliche, "a Bible that is falling apart is a sign of a life that isn't." The point is that if the physical text of your Bible is battered and dog-eared, held together with masking tape and so forth, that is a sign you have read it frequently and so are a faith-filled, committed Christian whom God will bless. I doubt any Sikh would agree with this sentiment, or the practice of writing or otherwise marking a sacred text. Even the (Anglo-) Catholic practice of reverencing the Gospel by kissing it might make a Sikh uncomfortable. It strikes me that Sikhs would be more comfortable with the Jewish practice of using a *yad* (literally "a hand"), to point to the text of a Torah scroll when reading it. The Muslim practice, of ensuring no other text is placed on top of the Qur'an, and that it has a place of particular honour within the house falls short of the reverence a Sikh would have for the Guru Granth Sahib, but it points in the right direction. For a Sikh, the Guru Granth Sahib is a living Guru, not an inanimate book at all. As a living Guru, the text must be treated appropriately, with due reverence and respect, cared for and loved as you would any honoured Guru.

In his discussion of doctrinal aspects of Sikhi, Ahluwalia is at pains to point out that while Christianity focuses its conception of the Word on the person of Jesus Christ, for Sikhs it is not the person of the Guru that is the focal point of faith, but his revelatory word. Thus, the Spirit becomes determinate in Word (*Gurbani*) not in the Guru. This means that the Guru Granth Sahib is understood as direct revelation by God himself to his Gurus; Gurus are merely the conduit through which the message is transmitted. The story of Guru Nanak being taken for three days into a vision of God's presence is therefore a way of indicating that he received direct revelation from God. Ahluwalia concludes:

> Among the sacred scriptures of the world Sri Guru Granth Sahib is unique in that it was compiled and authenticated by Guru Arjan, the fifth Prophet of Sikhism and acquired scriptural and

transcendental status – eternally living Guru – by a formal investiture of spiritual authority at the hands of Guru Gobind Singh, whereas the holy Books of other religions attained to this distinction only gradually through building up of tradition in the long course of time(2001, 36).

Christians and Sikhs may both say that God is One and that he is made known through his Word, but we mean radically different things when we make these two statements.

Satnam

The second phrase of the *mul mantar* is as problematic for translators as the first. Massey transliterates it as *satinamu*, and begins his discussion with a survey of possible translations:

- The true name is the creator
- There is but one God whose name is true
- The Eternal
- True is His name
- Of eternal manifestation
- His name is Truth
- He is the supreme Truth
- Reality, Reality of appearance, Truth manifest.

A CHRISTIAN'S THOUGHTS ABOUT *MUL MANTAR*

Noting the variety of positions translators take, Massey comments that a literal rendering does not do justice to the expression and so a study of Nanak's use of the term in other hymns is necessary to arrive at a sense of the meaning here (1991, 57-60).

Massey begins his survey by examining use of *sat*, citing four slokas:

1. In the beginning was Truth.
   In the beginning of the time was also Truth.
   Truth is now and will be also.

2. In the realm of Truth the Formless lives.

3. True is the Lord, true is the name.

4. There is always Truth, the Lord is true, and true is his name.

Truth is therefore the Being which always exists, which is understood as having no form. Truth is eternal, unchanging, without shape or physical existence.

Regarding *namu*, Massey also offers four slokas that illustrate its meaning:

1. As great is your creation, so great is your name.
   Without your name, there is no place.

2. Great is the Lord, high is his place.
   His name is highest above the high.

3. True is the Lord, true is the name.

4. The infinite name is unseeable and unknowable,
   But extremely sweet is the beloved name.

Satnam

This indicates that *namu* means more than just "name." In the first hymn it is linked with creation, in the second with the greatness of the Lord, in the third with truth and the fourth it is said to be infinite. Massey adds that *namu* is used in reference to "both historical and attributive names belonging to different religious and sectarian groups" (1991, 64), including Vaishnavite (such as Ram or Hari), non-Vaishnavite (such as Niranjanu) and Islamic (such as Khudai) names. Massey concludes that "*Namu* in a real sense represents the total nature of Reality (Truth) and when conjoined with *sati* in a single word, *satinamu*, it presents the conceptual aspect of Nanak's Ultimate Reality" (1991, 66).

Kaur Singh translates *Satnam* as "Truth by name," emphasising again the importance of avoiding gendered language in reference to Sikh concepts of the divine. Perhaps some of the translations Massey cites would be more accurate if masculine pronouns were avoided.

Kaur Singh discusses another text from the Guru Granth Sahib which reads:

> For the destitute, Your Name is wealth,
> For the homeless, Your Name is home,
> For the lowly, Your Name is honour,
> You grant Your gifts to every heart
> (AG 186, as cited in Kaur Singh 1995, 6).

Kaur Singh adds that every individual has the potential to be a sacred space for the Name, that each self can be "affirmed and celebrated as houses of the Divine, irrespective of gender, race, class and culture" (1995, 6). The Name is more than a marker of identity, it is the Divine. She cites another text which illustrates the point:

> Let us remember the Name and remind others
>   as well,

> By hearing, reciting and living the Name, we are liberated.
> The Name is the essence, the form and the reality;
> Says Nanak, let us praise the Name spontaneously.

Kaur Singh also notes that the Name is identified closely with the Word (*shabad*), another reference to the divine. Both the Name and the Word are "intangible and insubstantial, yet residing in the tangible and substantial"(1995, 7). The divine is all around us, present if not seen.

My reflections

True of Name or Truth by name. When I read this phrase, I am reminded of a theological concept found within Christianity, that the name indicates power. Thus, Christians pray in Jesus' name. This is exemplified in Peter's experience in Acts chapter 3. Peter and John go to the temple in Jerusalem to pray. As they enter the building by the "Beautiful Gate," they pass a beggar who asks for financial assistance. Peter replies, "I have no silver or gold, but what I have I give you; in the name of Jesus Christ of Nazareth, stand up and walk"(Acts 3:6). The man immediately stands up and walks. The crowd that witnesses this miracle immediately demand more information about this Jesus Christ of Nazareth. Peter preaches to them, and the number of believers increases to about five thousand (Acts 4:4). The incident causes such problems for the Temple authorities that Peter and John are arrested. This cycle of preaching and persecution continues for several chapters of the Acts of the Apostles. Peter and the other apostles preach boldly, and perform miracles. People begin to follow Jesus. The temple authorities, annoyed by these upstarts, arrest, threaten and beat Peter and his companions. As Luke summarises what has taken place, he writes:

> Then they [the temple authorities] ordered them [the Apostles] not to speak in the name of Jesus, and let them go. As they left the council, they rejoiced that they were considered worthy to suffer dishonour for the sake of the name. And every day in the temple and at home they did not cease to teach and proclaim Jesus as the Messiah (Acts 6:40-42, NRSV).

"Name" indicates character and power. Those who are faithful followers of Jesus are able to perform great miracles in Jesus' name. In Acts 19, particular emphasis is placed on the miracles that the Apostle Paul performs. But it is not enough to simply try to perform a miracle "in Jesus' name." This point is made clear in the episode of the seven sons of a Jewish High Priest named Sceva. They attempt exorcisms using the formula "I adjure you by the Jesus whom Paul proclaims" (Acts 19:13). An evil spirit responds to these sons "'Jesus I know, and Paul I know; but who are you?' Then the man with the evil spirit leapt on them, mastered them all, and so overpowered them that they fled out of the house naked and wounded" (Acts 19:15-16). The point is plain. It is not enough to know or speak the name. You must be in relationship with the one whose name is proclaimed, a teaching that holds for both Sikh and Christian expressions of faith.

There is also the question of truth. Jesus describes himself as "the way, and the truth, and the life" (John 14:6) and when he prays for his followers, reminds his father that he has "protected them in your name" (John 17:11) and urges his father to "sanctify them in the truth, your word is truth" (John 17:17). Many Christians hear this as urging a complete commitment and loyalty to Jesus as the only way of accessing the divine; others might counter this is simply the word of a guru to his disciples, demanding exclusive allegiance from those who have chosen to follow him.

Karta purakh

The translation challenges continue with the next phrase of the *mul mantar*. Massey, who anglicises the phrase as "*karata purakhu*," lists six examples of how it can be translated:

- The true name is the creator, the Spirit without fear

- Purusha, the creator

- Creator, Immanent Reality

- Creative His personality

- Creator (of existence) Lord

- A Purusha who is the creator.

Kaur Singh simply has "Primal Creator," again avoiding gendered language. She notes that Sikhi does not have fixed theories as to the origin of the universe, but that inclusion of the feminine within discussion of divine creation, then the model of motherly love, sensitivity for the environment and concerns for equality and justice come to the fore (2011, 61, 107).

Massey explains that in this instance, the particular challenge is in translating *purakhu*, which he notes is the Punjabi form of the Sanskrit term *purusha*, which itself can be translated in many ways, including "man, husband, ruler, Spirit, God, Lord, King." In order to understand how Guru Nanak uses the term, Massey cites four hymns:

Karta purakh

1. You O Creator *Purukhu*, who are inaccessible, you yourself have formed creation.

2. The True Guru has shown me the Primal *Purukhu* Who is different (from the creation) and is invisible.

3. The *Purukhu* himself is imperceptible and unmixed

4. You are the eternal *Purukhu* and death is not over your head. You are the incalculable *purukhu* (Being) and you are also inaccessible and unmixed.

In his analysis of these four hymns, Massey suggests that there is a clear relationship between *Karata* (Creator) and *Purukhu*, suggesting that *Karata Purukhu* refers to the cause of creation, who is also inaccessible. This point is repeated in the second hymn; the third suggests *Purukhu* is "imperceptible and unique," while the fourth that *Purukhu* is above death's power, cannot be calculated or accessed. Massey therefore concludes that Nanak uses *Purukhu* in the same way as he uses other names such as Allahu, the One God (1991, 90-92).

In their discussion of the Sikh understanding of the divine as creator, Cole and Sambhi explain that *Waheguru* never assumes physical form, whether animal or human. *Akal Purakh* is the creator, who willed the universe into being. They paraphrase a lengthy section of the Guru Granth Sahib that outlines the situation before time as follows:

> For millions of years there was nothing but darkness over the void. There was neither earth nor sky, only the Infinite Will. There was neither night not day, sun nor moon, and God was in a state of trance [*samadhi*]. The sources of creation did not exist, there was no speech, no air, no water, no birth, no death, no coming or going, no regions, no seven seas, no worlds above

or below. The *trimurti* of Brahma, Vishnu and Shiva did not exist. There was no other only the One. There was neither male nor female, *jati* or birth, pain or pleasure. There was no caste or religious garb, no brahmin or khatri. No Vedas or Muslim *kitab* existed, *smirts* or *shastras*. No reading of purana. No sunrise or sunset (AG 1035-6, cited in Cole and Sambhi 2006, 72).

No reason is given for why the divine chose to create; rather than discuss metaphysics, the Guru is only interested in the experience of creation. Cole and Sambhi offer the following translation:

The Infinite One's might became enshrined within all but God is detached and without limit or equal. In creation nature and inanimate nature came for the existing void. From God's Being [*sunte*] came air, water and the world, bodies and the divine spirit with them. Your light is within fire, water and living beings and in your Absolute Self lies the power of creation.

From the Absolute emanated Brahma, Vishnu and Shiva: from God come all the ages ...

All that springs from God merges with God again. By God's play the nature has been created and by the *shabad* the wonder has become manifest.

From God's own Being has come day and night, creation and destruction, pleasure and pain.

The godly-minded remain stable and detached from the effect of good or ill and find their home in God.
(AG 1037, cited in Cole and Sambhi 2006, 72).

Thus, all that exists emanates from the divine and will one day return to the divine. There are no real concerns about the mechanism involved and so Sikhs have no problem with evolution, but do disagree with "materialism which regards the universe as self-explanatory and self-existent" (Cole and Sambhi 2006, 72-73).

In his discussion of Guru Nanak's teaching that material reality is the creation of *Karta Purakh*, Ahluwalia explains that the Guru's doctrine meant that time and space were no longer understood as accidental in origin or lacking purpose. Rather, there was clarity – human beings could form a relationship with God, and their relationships with each other were also of significant importance. Doctrine is not just abstract belief, but has a real impact on how society is organised and functions. Equally, the idea of the unity of the divine (*Ik Omkar*) is not just a theological concept, but entails a rejection of a hierarchical society, for if *Karta Purakh* is one, all can relate to the divine equally, and a rigid caste system is of no meaning or value. The point is that God is one, but there are many paths of approach. This means society should be pluralistic and egalitarian (1999, 51-54).

My reflections

As noted in the section on Manifest as Word above, within the Christian understanding, Jesus is the one in whom and through whom creation took place. The Apostle Paul summarises his understanding as follows:

> He is the image of the invisible God, the first-born of all creation; for in him all things in heaven and on earth were created, things visible and invisible, whether thrones or dominions or rulers or powers—all things have been created through him and for him. He himself is before

A CHRISTIAN'S THOUGHTS ABOUT *MUL MANTAR*

> all things, and in him all things hold together. He is the head of the body, the church; he is the beginning, the firstborn from the dead, so that he might come to have first place in everything. For in him all the fullness of God was pleased to dwell, and through him God was pleased to reconcile to himself all things, whether on earth or in heaven, by making peace through the blood of his cross (Colossians 1:15-20, NRSV).

Paul's point is similar to that made in the opening verses of John's Gospel, namely that Jesus is the origin and source of creation. The phrase "in him all things hold together" reminds us that Jesus is also understood to be the one who sustains creation, and the reference to Jesus' death and resurrection emphasises the fact that Jesus is the means by which humanity, and all creation, enters into and maintains relationship with God.

Christianity emphasises both the immanence and the transcendence of God. The Father is seen as sovereign and transcendent, above and outside of creation. The Son (and the Spirit) are understood as immanent, present and involved in every aspect of creation. The early Church Father Irenaeus summed this up by describing the Son and the Spirit as the "two hands" of God, upholding and sustaining the created order. This is a metaphorical, not a physical description, but nevertheless indicates how the distinction between the Creator and the creation is maintained. For Christianity, it is important that God is distinct from and outside of creation; the doctrinal arguments of the first few centuries of Christianity were won by those who argued that Jesus, the Son, was distinct from creation, that he is eternally self-existent and is the Word through whom creation was spoken into being.

Nirbhau, nirvair

Massey discusses the next two terms, *nirbhau* and *nirvair* together, explaining they are both negative terms that are normally used together by Guru Nanak. Massey presents five translations, all of which are similar:

- Without fear, without enmity
- Devoid of fear and enmity
- Without fear, without hate
- Without fear and enmity
- Without fear, without Rancour.

While most agree with this approach, Massey notes that a minority of translators do suggest that *nirbhau* has been misunderstood. Guru Iqbal Singh argues that *nirbhau* should actually be derived from the root *bhav*, which means "becoming." Thus *nirabhau* means "becominglessness," that is to say, it indicates the divine is without birth or death, origin or end. Massey himself rejects this interpretation, siding with the majority opinion that "fearless" is the correct interpretation. The point is that one should live in *bhai*, fear of the Lord, in order to become without fear (Massey 1991, 93-97).

Cole and Sambhi explain that the statement that God is fearless and without hatred is a deliberate contrast with Hindu mythology, where gods are sometimes portrayed as afraid and so engaging in tricks and vindictive wars. There is also a contrast with human beings who are regularly afraid and consumed by hatred. Once a Sikh finds union with the divine, all these issues are dealt with: "The Guru's servants are pleasing to God who forgives them and they no longer fear death's courier. God dispels the doubt of devotees, enjoying union with them. Free from fear, limitless and infinite the creator is pleased with truth" (AG 1190 cited in Cole and Sambhi 2006, 73).

A CHRISTIAN'S THOUGHTS ABOUT *MUL MANTAR*

My reflections

Fear is a corrosive and divisive force, a powerful emotion that drives us to respond from our most basic, primal instincts. When we feel threatened, reason or logic are no longer persuasive; the "fight, flight or freeze" response is evoked, and whichever is chosen, damage to self and others is the likely result. In 1 John, we read that "There is no fear in love, but perfect love casts out fear; for fear has to do with punishment, and whoever fears has not reached perfection in love" (1 John 4:18). A few verses earlier, John also writes that "God is love, and those that abide in love abide in God, and God abides in them" (1 John 4:16). The argument is clear; agreeing with the *mul mantar*, 1 John argues that there is no fear within the divine and that by extension those who are fully committed to, and immersed in, the divine will themselves not experience fear.

Arguing that the true believer will not experience fear is a bold statement that is perhaps at odds with the reality of the Biblical record. The command "do not fear" is a common one, often found on the lips of angels or of Jesus himself. The opening chapters of Matthew and Luke, the two Gospels that record the birth narratives of Jesus, contain a number of scenes when an angel brings a message from God, but the first words spoken are a command to not fear. Similarly, when Jesus walks on water, his disciples are afraid, and Jesus reassures them that there is no need to fear because he is present. The phrase he uses, "it is I," or "I am" echoes the divine name in the original Greek of the text, returning us to the point that there is no fear within God (John 6:20).

When Moses gathers the people of God at the foot of Mount Sinai, and the presence of God descends on the mountain with thunder and lightning and smoke, the people are afraid. Moses tells them they do not need to fear, because God has come "only to test you and to put the fear of him upon you so that you do not sin" (Exodus 20:20). People of faith do not tend to talk today of the importance of fearing God, yet there are instructions to do so within the Hebrew scriptures. The book of Proverbs explains that "the fear of the Lord is the beginning of knowledge; fools despise wisdom and instruction" (Proverbs 1:7). This point is developed further in other texts, for example that "the fear of the Lord is hatred of evil" (Proverbs 8:13) and that "the fear of the Lord is the beginning of wisdom, and the knowledge of the Holy One is insight" (Proverbs 9:10). A very specific type of fear, the fear of God, is thus understood in a positive sense. While at first sight it may seem incongruous to argue that there is no fear in God, but that God must be feared, there is, in fact, a synergy between these two positions as the fear of the Lord is arguably quite different from the fear that is not present in God. The former can be understood in the sense of awe, while the latter in the sense of terror. The expectation is therefore that personal and corporate behaviour is shaped by a recognition of human finitude in contrast with the infinity of God. For those who are in a good relationship with God this can be a positive experience in the sense of shaping behaviour, both what is actively embraced and what is deliberately shunned.

There are instances within the Hebrew scriptures when God describes the things that he hates. Through the Prophet Malachi, God rebukes those who are being unfaithful to their spouses and says that he hates both divorce and "covering one's garment with violence" (Malachi 2:16). The Prophet Isaiah records God's hatred of the festivals practised by the people (Isaiah 1:14) and of "robbery and wrongdoing" (Isaiah 61:8). In Amos, we hear God say:

> I hate, I despise your festivals,
>> and I take no delight in your solemn assemblies.
> Even though you offer me your burnt-offerings
>> and grain-offerings,

> I will not accept them;
> and the offerings of well-being of your fatted animals
> I will not look upon.
> Take away from me the noise of your songs;
> I will not listen to the melody of your harps.
> But let justice roll down like waters,
> and righteousness like an ever-flowing stream.
> (Amos 5:21-24, NRSV).

These, and other passages like them, suggest that God has standards, that there are attitudes and actions which are detestable and which cannot be sanctioned. Within the New Testament, Jesus is similarly vitriolic in his condemnation of religious hypocrisy; his diatribe against the Pharisees in Matthew 23:1-36 is perhaps the longest and clearest example. But there are other texts as well; Jesus rebukes his own close followers for excluding children (Luke 18:15-17), as well as turning over the tables of the money changers in the temple (Mark 11:15-19 and parallels; John 2:13-25).

The relationship between this hatred of wrong doing and enmity needs unpacking. If we understand enmity in a sense of baseless antagonism, a prejudicial hatred of someone because of who they are, then I can concur that God is without enmity. It is a cliche to say that God loves the sinner while hating the sin, but the underlying presumption, that no one is, in and of themselves, rejected by God is foundational to a Christian worldview. Christians remain in awe of God because he is without enmity or prejudice but loves and disciplines all people equally.

Akal murat

When he discusses the phrase *Akal murat*, Massey notes that translations differ depending on whether the emphasis is

Akal murat

on the former or the latter word. If it is the latter, then translations such as "immortal," "a Being whom Death cannot assail," and "Whose form is away from death," are used. But if the focus is on *akal*, then translations such as "Timeless form," "The Being beyond time," and "Having a timeless form" are used (1991, 97-98). Massey suggests that the term *murat* within the *mul mantar* is used to indicate the fact that *Ik Omkar*'s form is subtle, imperceptible to the senses, but can be experienced through the material world. Massey's exploration of the meaning of the adjective *akal* focuses on the problem of referring to "timelessness," for Massey suggests that the issue is not so much time as creation; the point is that the divine is self-established and self-created, with unchangeable form, the only firm reality, the eternal one. The point Guru Nanak is making is that the divine is outside the temporal realm (Massey 1991, 99-103). Thus Kaur Singh translates the opening *shalok*, which is between the *mul mantar* and the rest of *Japji* as follows:

> Truth before time
> Truth throughout time
> Truth here and now
> Says Nanak, Truth is evermore (1995, 51).

Ahluwalia explores the concept of timelessness at length. He argues that if a being is described as timeless, then this is often thought to mean that it is "not subject to the temporal processes of origination, development and disintegration." Within Indian philosophical thought, this concept is encapsulated in the understanding of the "primary noumenal substance which alone is the Real (*sat*) in the sense of eternal, timeless, ever-same Being in relation to which the world of becoming has either derivative reality, or no reality at all." Within the Sikh concept of time, human beings are understood to be on an upward evolutionary and developmental trajectory as this quote from Guru Arjan demonstrates:

A CHRISTIAN'S THOUGHTS ABOUT *MUL MANTAR*

> For several births you were just a worm
> For several births, an elephant, a fish, a deer
> For several births a bird, a serpent
> For several births served as a bull, horse
> This is the moment of union with God –
> Now that you have, after ages, evolved into the human form.
> Many times destroyed in the womb
> For countless times subjected to vegetative growth
> Passing through myriads of species
> Through communion with the Holy you arose into a man
> Serve now the Lord, meditating on the Guru's word (Ahluwalia 1999, 42).

The idea is also found in *Japji*, where the five successive stages (*khands*) of a person are set out, culminating in the spiritual union of a person to God. Pashaura Singh outlines the five stages in detail explaining that the *Japji* describes ascent through the five mystical realms. First is the realm of duty (*dharam khand*), the law of cause and effect operates as one lives in the world and is judged by the actions one takes in the world. Second is the realm of knowledge (*gian khand*), marked by experiences of awe through widening of one's intellectual horizons in appreciation of the vastness of the universe, and at the same time shattering one's self-centred pride. The third realm is the realm of effort (*saram khand*), where human faculties and sensibilities are beautified by means of the divine Word. The fourth stage, the realm of grace (*karam khand*), is where the power and authority of the divine word is established in the mystic's life. The fifth, and final, stage is the realm of truth (*sach khand*), where the soul of the mystic finds union with the "Formless one"(*nirankar*), with the Word that is the voice of *Akal Purakh*. Overall, the focus is on establishing complete harmony with the divine command, as the mystic becomes an agent of the divine will (2016, 231-34).

God is not understood as timeless within time, but rather as time-transcendent, as encapsulated in the concept of *Akal murat*. As in Biblical thought, time is understood to have begun once reality was created: "God as *Karta Purakh* created not only the world, but also time as the mode or the constitutive aspect of the phenomenal reality" (Ahluwalia 1999, 44).

This means that the "keynote concept" of *Akal murat* indicates that God is transcendent above time in two senses, both of logical priority and of historical priority. This is different from the Vedantic understanding – and Ahluwalia's point is that many translators and interpreters of the *Mul Mantar* fail to recognise the need to make this distinction. Within a Vedantic understanding, the divine is not creator, because there is no time when creation did not exist. But in the *Mul Mantar*, it is clear that God is supra-temporal(*Akal murat*) but also the Creative spirit who fashioned everything, including time (*Karta Purakh*). The divine is not simply abstract Infinity, but determinate Infinity, and the created order is a determination of the Absolute.

Guru Nanak's explanation of the divine is thus deliberately cast in contra-distinction to both Vedantic (Hindu) and Buddhist understandings, and any attempt to translate the text must reflect this. Ahluwalia therefore argues that the term *Sat Nam* does not mean "his Name is Truth" or "His reality is eternal," but rather "His Name (*qua* determinate Infinity) is True." That is to say, the phrase *Sat Nam* "emphasises the reality of the (relational) determinate aspect of the Absolute," just as the phrase *Ik Omkar* emphasises the "in-itself indeterminacy and abstractedness of the Absolute." The ultimate Reality is not entirely abstract, but real, concrete and active within time (Ahluwalia 1999, 39-49).

A CHRISTIAN'S THOUGHTS ABOUT *MUL MANTAR*

Ajuni, saibhang

Massey examines *Ajuni saibhang* as a phrase, beginning with a discussion of the word *ajuni*. A wide range of translations are offered, including "unborn," "without reason or cause," "not produced from the womb," "one who does not take birth, not-incarnated," and "one who is free from transmigration." The breadth of possible translations necessitates a detailed discussion, which is summarised here. Massey begins with reference to the related Sanskrit term *ayoni*, where *a-* is a negative prefix and *yoni* means womb, vagina, any place of birth or origin, any generating cause, or a family, stock, race, birth, or form of existence. A similar meaning is found in Punjabi. A further complication comes from the fact that in the *mul mantar*, the spelling *ajuni* is used, but elsewhere, Guru Nanak has *ajoni*; this latter spelling is particularly influential on the translation that focuses on transmigration of souls. Massey adds that *ajoni* indicates one who has no generating cause. This concept is not easily translated into English. It is preferable, Massey proposes, to have an explanation that the divine did not come into being or existence through the natural process of birth or through the womb or from a mother or father. The addition of *Saibhang* should add some clarification, as most translate is "self-existent." The point is that the divine is self-caused, rather than caused by any other (1991, 103-11).

Massey discusses the conception of the divine as Creator in detail, as there are hymns throughout the Adi Granth that extol the Creator at length. Guru Nanak uses different metaphors and ideas to explain how creation came into being. One of these is the phrase *dhundhukara,* which is variously translated as "deep darkness," "utter darkness," or "chaos," with an implied meaning "non-existence" or "nothingness," making it clear that the Creator manifested himself from the unmanifest, from nothing. The second phrase, *sunnu,* was used in Buddhist thought to indicate the Void or

Ajuni, saibhang

of an uncaused reality at the origin of creation. Massey is clear that this is contrary to Guru Nanak's thought; for the Guru, *sunnu* is understood in terms of the Absolute Self, the uncaused cause of creation. The third term, *andaja,* means "egg." Massey suggests this indicates Guru Nanak using terminology familiar to his first audience. The idea of the Creator emerging from a golden egg and then creating all was a common creation myth at the time. Massey argues that Guru Nanak co-opts the language, without embracing this myth, as he has elsewhere rejected the idea of the divine using pre-existent matter to shape creation. In these and his other hymns, Guru Nanak makes it clear that *Waheguru* created according to a divine timescale, for divine purposes, for the saints to practice righteousness and so that people might serve their Maker. The main point is that the Creator made and is therefore sovereign (1991, 113-28).

Cole and Sambhi explain that the statement in the *mul mantar* that God is *ajuni*, without birth, is only necessary because Sikhi developed in a predominantly Hindu environment, where the doctrine of avatar was held (2006, 95). For example in the Bhagavad Gita, Krishna explains the circumstances which cause him to arise and to descend on the world:

> Whenever there is a decline in *dharma*, O Bharata, and whenever there is an increase in *adharma*, it is then that I manifest myself. For the protection of the righteous (*sadhus*), for the destruction of the wrongdoers and for the purpose of establishing dharma, I appear age after age. He who fully understands the truth about my divine birth and activity does not take birth again after giving up his body. He comes to Me, Arjuna. (Bhagavad Gita 4:7-9, Nicholas Sutton's translation).

But for Sikhs, Waheguru is *nirguna*, without qualities. Thus, the divine is manifested not physically, "but as Truth, as Word, as Name." Moreover, Waheguru is continually active, revealing divinity and sustaining creation. In the Sikh perspective, an avatar of the divine suggests "not a caring God who restores order when the need arises, but a casual one who lets things slide and then is compelled reluctantly to intervene" (Cole and Sambhi 2006, 95). That is not to say that the divine has not communicated through Moses or Jesus or Muhammad, but rather than none brought definitive or final revelation. As Kaur Singh explains, "The One does not impose a scripture or specify a mode of thought; but rather, its very being consists in the many" (2011, 62). All revelations and scriptures that speak of the divine are therefore respected and affirmed.

My reflections

I will discuss the final three phrases, Whose Form is Infinite, Unborn, Self-Existent, together, in order to avoid unnecessary repetition. One of my favourite songs about the incarnation is *We worship a wonderful saviour* by Joel Payne. The song includes the lines "In the form of this child is the fulness of God. His infinity hides in his weakness. His divinity beats in his human heart." The Christian understanding of God includes the idea that God is both infinite, but also finite, both unborn, but also born, both self-existent but also brought into human existence through a virgin birth.

At one level, the Christian understanding of God therefore corresponds closely with the Sikh understanding described here. God exists outside of time, with no beginning and no end. The opening verses of the Bible are argued by some to indicate precisely this point, that God, distinct from creation, chose to bring creation into being. Moreover, in his letter to the Romans, Paul writes of God as the one "who gives life to the dead and calls into existence the things that do not exist" (Romans 4:17). This phrase is traditionally understood by Christians as teaching that God created everything out of nothing.

The Apostolic creed of the Christian church describes Jesus as being "begotten not made, of one being with the Father." A Christian Trinitarian understanding of God would argue that God has been eternally in relationship with God's self, which means that God has always existed as Father, Son and Holy Spirit. But at a particular time, God became finite, born, existing in dependance on others, when Jesus Christ appeared. Jesus was born in human likeness, but he was not created by God.

The Apostle Paul summarises the point by explaining that Jesus

> Who, though he was in the form of God, did not regard equality with God as something to be exploited, but emptied himself, taking the form of a slave, being born in human likeness (Philippians 2:6-7, NRSV).

The finitude of God in Jesus is important to Christianity. It allows the book of Hebrews to describe Jesus as one who has been tested (or tempted) in every way as all human beings are, yet without sin (Hebrews 4:15). This personal experience allows Jesus to empathise with the struggles of sinful humanity, and so gives the believer in Christ confidence to approach him in prayer when facing personal difficulties or challenges. The understanding that in Jesus God took on human form is arguably one of the key differences between Sikhi and Christianity and therefore is worthy of serious discussion and exploration.

A CHRISTIAN'S THOUGHTS ABOUT *MUL MANTAR*

Gurprasad

Massey explains that the final phrase of the *mul mantar* has been translated variously as:

- By the favour of the Guru
- By the Grace of One Supreme Being
- Realised by the grace of the Holy Preceptor
- Through the Grace of His true servant, continually repeat His name
- By His grace shalt thou worship Him.

It is a challenging phrase to understand, and Massey examines it in stages, beginning with *gur*. The traditional understanding is the *gur* is made up of two roots, *gu* meaning "darkness" and *ru* meaning "remover"(or as "light" in popular usage); hence a *gur* or *guru* is the one who removes darkness or ignorance. A second understanding is that there is a link to the Sanskrit noun *gri*, which means "to swallow, to make understand." Hence the *guru* is one who swallows up ignorance and makes one understand real wisdom.

The second key question is the identity of this *gur*. This was a question Nanak was asked in his own lifetime. He replied that his *guru* was the Word, *Ik Omkaru* himself, a point made repeatedly by Guru Nanak in his hymns. At the same time, Guru Nanak also stresses that while there may be other human teachers, even these are all One. Moreover, even nature is a teacher. In the closing *slokas* of *Japji*, he writes: "Air is Guru, the Father is water, the Mother is earth..." But while nature can be encountered anywhere, encounter with the Lord is entirely a result of his grace, his merciful glance. Those who receive this grace are truly blessed as they encounter the divine.

Gurprasad

The term *parasadi* means "by the favour, the grace (of)," although other idiomatic uses are also recognised, such as *parasada Sakana*, to take food, or *parasada sukhana*, to make a commitment for a special offering. Guru Nanak's focus at the end of the *mul mantar* is to emphasise that revelation of the divine only comes about through the self-expression or self-communication of *Ik Omkar*(Massey 1991, 129-55). McLeod questions whether "grace" is the best term because of the implications from Christian theology of "the specific Pauline doctrine of grace with its stress upon the universal nature of grace and of its absolute sufficiency for salvation." McLeod is also cautious about "election," which he regards as coming close to Nanak's meaning, but is problematic for being "too closely associated with neo-Calvinist theology" and the belief in "double predestination" of some to salvation and others to damnation. McLeod also rejects "favour" and "choice" as lacking sufficient depth of meaning, and so reluctantly concludes that "grace" is the best English translation of the gift of perception and illumination that allows the possibility of a disciple to accept revelation, live in conformity with that revelation and so move towards union with the divine (1968, 206).

Parry discusses contrasting theories of grace, explaining that in North India the "monkey-hold doctrine of grace is commonly held." He elaborates that when a tribe of monkeys faces danger, a baby monkey runs and holds on to its mother for protection. In the same way, Parry says Sikhs believe that human beings must take the first step towards the divine to encounter grace. By contrast, Christians tend to have a "cat-hold doctrine of grace," which uses the fact that mother cats tend to take the initiative and lift their kittens by the scruff of the neck, so God takes the first step in searching out his people, both deserving and undeserving (2009, 96). I will return to this point when discussing Parry's reflections at greater length in a subsequent chapter.

A CHRISTIAN'S THOUGHTS ABOUT *MUL MANTAR*

Cole and Sambhi explain the Sikh conception of grace through a description of how students wait for their guru's pleasure:

> Outside the guru's home the faithful and the hopeful will sit and wait for him to appear (most gurus are male). He may be away from the village in which case they will remain until his return. When he does appear there need be no words, merely a benign look of acceptance that is enough to convey a blessing. That glance is darshan. It is this that Sikhism has in mind when it speaks of God's grace. God is the supreme Guru. Experience teaches that some people make the hard journey of asceticism or moral effort but do not receive this glance of acceptance. Others with but little struggle are not only smiled upon, they are initiated into the close fellowship of disciples (2006, 80).

This is not an arbitrary or fickle action of the divine, but rather it is a pronouncement from the supreme Guru who knows best what every individual needs. This point is illustrated through quotations from the Guru Granth Sahib:

> All bounties come from God. No one can claim them as a matter of right. Some who are awake do not receive them, others are roused from their slumbers to be blessed (AG 83).

> Good actions may precure a better existence, but liberation comes only from grace (AG 2).

> God cannot be understood or realized through cleverness (AG 221, all cited in Cole and Sambhi 2006, 80).

Thus, for Sikhs, grace is the special notice that Waheguru takes of a person; it may even be a displeased glance, whose consequences are disastrous. Whatever is given, good or bad, flows from the infinite wisdom and mercy of the divine.

Cole and Sambhi conclude their discussion of the understanding of grace within Sikh by summarising that grace is

> the glance which a Guru bestows upon the disciple denoting acceptance and conveying a blessing. It is also a glance which liberates the devotee in such a way that the efforts which were once undertaken to win recognition are now acts of loving service. Grace also transforms the disciple from being a hopeful seeker to being someone who has found the meaning of personal existence and is now at peace, having realized God (2006, 81-82).

Sondhi concurs with Cole and Sambhi that grace in Sikhi is understood as receipt of the divine glance. Sondhi suggests that the experience of prayer, especially recitation of the divine name, elicits a quickening of the devotee's entire being, which allows divine grace to settle in the heart. This in turn means that the works of grace manifest themselves, and the devotee no longer vacillates between right and wrong, good and evil, but is drawn inexorably along the divine path. Thus, Sondhi asks, "How can a man who is committed to the Name, or to a God of love and purity, and who looks on Him as the source of whatever measure of these excellences is there in his own being, fall a prey to transgressions of sense, impurity in thought, and anger in speech?" (2002, 22). Once grace is at work in the believer's heart, the implication is therefore that purification of life naturally follows. Whilst grace is available to all, only the devoted attain it; it is the intensity of their devotion that enables them to realise the grace of God (2002, 33). The way to attain grace is therefore to let go of worldly attachment, and begin the inner journey of devotion towards the supreme being.

My reflections

Christians would concur that faith is a gift of God, that everything we have is a result of his grace which flows particularly from the life, death and resurrection of Jesus Christ. Indeed, there is a popular mnemonic that illustrates this, defining grace as God's Riches At Christ's Expense. Parry's suggestion that the Christian understanding of grace is an active one is also something I resonate with; as Paul explains to the Romans, "God proves his love for us in that while we still were sinners Christ died for us"(Romans 5:8). The point is that God takes the initiative in reconciling his people to himself. Everything the Christian does, living a life of worship, is therefore supposed to be an overflow of gratitude for the grace which has been received. To quote the Christian song writer Stuart Townend:

> 'Cause it's grace.
> There's nothing I can do
> To make You love me more,
> To make You love me less than You do.
> And by faith
> I'm standing on this Stone
> Of Christ and Christ alone,
> Your righteousness is all that I need,
> 'Cause it's grace.

This point is repeatedly emphasised within Christian scripture. A second example is found in Paul's letter to the Ephesians, where he explains that it is "by grace you have been saved through faith, and this is not your own doing; it is the gift of God – not the result of works, so that no one may boast" (Ephesians 2:8-9, NRSV). A foundational teaching within Christian faith is that acts of devotion, service and worship are responses to the grace of God as revealed in Christ; they are not a way to earn God's favour, but our grateful response to what has already been received.

Chapter 3

A Christian's Reflections on reading Japji

Shackle and Mandair explain:

> Guru Nanak's *Japji* is, without question, the greatest of all the many compositions which are contained in the Sikh scriptures. This special status is reflected in the honorific *-ji* which is commonly added to the name *Jap* or 'Recitation'. It is printed at the beginning of the Adi Granth, on pp.1-8. It also appears at the beginning of private prayer books, since it is prescribed for daily recitation by all devout Sikhs in the early morning (*amrit vela*) (2005, 1).

They add that the text is written to be recited as a litany, which contrasts with most of the Adi Granth, which is written to be sung, and so is arranged according to the different

A CHRISTIAN'S REFLECTIONS ON READING JAPJI

ragas. The language used is complex; combining Old Hindu and Old Punjabi with technical language in Sanskrit and Persian. The *Japji* regularly uses anaphora, repeating the same word or phrase at the start of successive lines. The text is not necessarily full grammatical sentences, often containing simply nouns and names. The pace at which the *Japji* is recited changes as the text is spoken; a variety of metres and patterns are used, as the stanzas lengthen and shorten.

Shackle and Mandair describe the *Japji* as "the work of Guru Nanak's maturity" (2005, 2) and argue it is centred around praise of the unknowable divinity as it sets out the core themes of the Guru Granth Sahib. The *Japji* begins with the *mul mantar*, discussed above, and then continues with an introductory *shalok* and then thirty-eight stanzas, whose content and arrangement Shackle and Mandair summarise as follows. First, *hukam*, the need to follow the divine will and command. Second, a list of the divine commands and their effects. Third, a list of those who praise the divine, who is indescribable. Fourth, praise of the divine and the Name. Fifth, praise of the divine, with refrain A, an invocation to the Guru. Sixth, praise of the Guru's teachings, with refrain A. Seventh, it is impossible for human beings to describe the divine. Stanzas eight to eleven list what results from listening to the Name, with refrain B, which details the blessings of the Name. Stanzas twelve to fifteen list the results of acceptance, with refrain C, how the Name is known through acceptance. Sixteen gives praise of saints and the divine power, and refrain D, that God, the Formless One, cannot be described. Stanza seventeen lists the innumerable good people, with refrain D. Eighteen lists the innumerable bad people, also with refrain D. Nineteen covers the nature of unknowable divinity, with refrain D. Stanza twenty explains how the Name has power to save, and how people are responsible for their actions. Twenty-one, that the moment of creation cannot be known. Twenty-two, that scripture cannot describe creation. Twenty-three, that praise is not enough and that material wealth is of lesser importance than devotion. Stanza twenty-four, that the divine surpasses any human efforts at praise. Twenty-five, that God is infinitely bountiful. Twenty-six, a list of divine attributes. Twenty-seven is a hymn that lists all those who praise the divine. Twenty-eight sets out what makes a true yogi, and has refrain E, praise to the Primal Being. Stanzas twenty-nine to thirty-one celebrate the power of the divine, with refrain E. Thirty-two says that humans cannot describe the divine. Thirty-three, that everything which occurs does so because of the divine will. Thirty-four, where righteous action takes place. Stanzas thirty-five and thirty-six cover the realm of wisdom. Thirty-seven speaks of the realm of action and truth. Thirty-eight summarises the spiritual discipline needed if divine favour is to lead to spiritual transformation. The *Japji* then concludes with a final, unnumbered, *shalok* (2005, 2-3).

The only way to really engage properly with the *Japji* is to read it through. In what follows, I have reproduced the translation of Shackle and Mandair (2005, 4-19), largely according to the divisions they identify. It has some limitations, notably the use of gendered language, and I will also refer to Kaur Singh's translations where that becomes an issue. The focus of the discussion is on how I as a Christian react to what I read. It is therefore a highly subjective response to a particular Sikh text. Doubtless there will be passages that I misunderstand; I hope that nothing I write is offensive. The purpose is to open up a conversation about what this most important of Sikh texts means to people of faith today.

The opening *shalok* reads:

> True in the beginning, True before time began,
> He is True, Nanak, and ever will be True.

This makes me think of the prologue to John's Gospel, the idea discussed in the previous chapter, of the eternal Word

A CHRISTIAN'S REFLECTIONS ON READING JAPJI

dwelling with the divine from before the time creation was brought into existence. Jesus also describes himself as "the Truth" in his dialogue with his disciples before his final night on earth (John 14:6). Religious faith is based on the understanding that what is believed is true. For some truth can be relative, but for others – including myself – truth is understood in a more exclusive, absolute sense. Truth demands a response of loyalty and wholehearted commitment.

Stanza one:

> No idea of Him can be conceived through thousands of thoughts,
> Ultimate silence evades the most deep meditation.
> To heap up the wealth of the world does not lessen man's hunger,
> And multiple cleverness will not assist us hereafter.
> Nanak says: How to be cleared? How to break down the wall of the ego? –
> Follow His will and command, from the first written out.

Kaur Singh's translation is:

> Thought cannot think, nor can a million thoughts.
> Silence cannot silence, nor can seamless contemplation.
> Greed is not made greedless, not by the wealth of all the world.
> Though a thousand mental feats become a million, not one can go with us.
> How then to be true? How then to break the wall of lies?
> By following the Will. Says Nanak, this is written for us.
> (1995, 51-52).

Stanza one

The idea of God being ineffable, unapproachable, beyond human understanding, does have a place in Christian theology. There is a tradition within scholastic thinking in particular which makes much of the fact that God cannot be fully known – the so called "apophatic tradition." This same notion is found within the Hebrew scriptures. In the book of Isaiah, for example, the Lord says:

> For my thoughts are not your thoughts,
>   nor are your ways my ways, says the Lord.
> For as the heavens are higher than the earth,
>   so are my ways higher than your ways
>   and my thoughts than your thoughts (Isaiah 55:8-9, NRSV)

The point is that human beings can never hope to attain understanding of the divine; the best we can hope for is a very partial glimpse, a small amount of understanding. For a Sikh, the emphasis is therefore very much on experiencing Waheguru.

Shackle and Mandair note that an alternative translation for the first line would be "Ultimate purity cannot be found in thousands of cleansings." This reminds us that whatever it is we try to do as human beings, we are not able to come close to God. The only way humans and the divine can connect is through divine initiative. For a Christian, this initiative is expressed most clearly in the incarnation, the belief in God in human flesh, God knowable, personal, relatable, the infinite become finite within creation in the person of Jesus. For a Sikh, this opening stanza suggests that obedience to the divine commands will result in establishing a relationship where Waheguru can draw closer to the believer.

A CHRISTIAN'S REFLECTIONS ON READING JAPJI

Stanza two:

> By the command, forms are produced,
> But the command cannot be defined.
> By the command, creatures exist,
> By the command, greatness is gained.
> By the command, men are made high and made low,
> By the command, sorrows and joys are received.
> By the command, some are granted His favour,
> By the command, some must forever revolve.
> All are within the command,
> Outside of it no one can live.
> Nanak, to grasp the command
> Is to renounce ego-sense.

The idea behind this second stanza, that of *hukam*, the nature, divine order of things, is one that is also found within Christian theology. In this context, I think especially of divine providence, that God orders and controls all things. The biblical text that most resonates for me is the book of Ecclesiastes, especially the meditation on the right time for things, in chapter three. I wonder what a Sikh would make of the conclusion Qohelet, the teacher of Ecclesiastes, reaches, that in the end of the matter, the only thing to do is fear God and honour the king? (Ecclesiastes 12:13-14).

A second point is that of election and whether God predestines people, some to destruction and others to eternal life. Christians have very mixed views on this, some arguing that the notion of free will means that people always have a choice. Others believe that divine sovereignty over everything means that ultimately God is in charge of all that happens, including predestination for eternity with or eternal separation from God (what is conventionally termed heaven and hell).

Stanza three

Stanza three:

> Some sing of His power, for they have the power,
> Some sing of His bounty, for they know its signs.
>
> Some sing of His virtues, greatness and acts,
> Some sing of His knowledge, so hard to imagine,
> Some sing of His making, the body, then dust,
> Some sing of His taking, and giving back life.
> Some sing that He seems and appears far away,
> Some sing that He sees all, present and here.
> In His description, no shortfall is found
> As millions try over and over again.
> He never stops giving, the takers get tired,
> Throughout all the ages, they feed and they feed.
> Through this command, it is the command that lays out the way.
> Nanak, free from all care He rejoices.

We internalise our faith through our songs, as well as forming doctrine; it is striking that Shackle and Mandair's translation is gendered, whilst Kaur Singh's is not. Her translation begins "Filled with might, they sing praise of the Mighty" and continues in the same vein (1995, 52).

One of the tragedies of the lockdowns that resulted from the COVID-19 pandemic was that people of faith were unable to meet and sing together. If we could not sing any more, what had our worship become? A mere, dry formulation? Worthless words? One of the most powerful Psalms, Psalm 137, is a lament of the people of Israel, who are unable to sing the Lord's song in a strange land. During the lockdowns, Christians ended up singing the Lord's song in the strange land of self-isolation. Sikhs equally could not gather for *kirtan*. The question remains: can I truly praise the divine if I sing alone?

A CHRISTIAN'S REFLECTIONS ON READING JAPJI

Christian songs, even those in the scriptures, fall short of fully describing the majesty and greatness of God. The themes echo those of section two, but their beauty is enhanced by being put to music. We try as best we can to put the majesty of God into words, but even though there are beautiful passages of Scripture, for example Paul's hymn in Philippians 2 or Colossians 1, or John's description of the Word in the Prologue to his Gospel, yet still these words all fall short. Relationship with God is so personal, so intimate, that words alone cannot describe it.

Stanza four:

> The Lord is True, and True in Name,
> Whose speech is love that has no limit.
> They beg and ask, 'O give, O give'
> The Giver then bestows His bounty.
> What can be offered in return
> To gain the prospect of His court?
> What words to be expressed are there,
> To cause Him to bestow His love?
> Before the dawn reflect upon
> The greatness of the Name that's True.
> Through deeds we've done we get this garment,
> Through grace we reach salvation's gate.
> Nanak, it must be realised
> That of Himself He's All and True.

This hymn of praise to the Name speaks to me of love. What does it mean to love? As Jesus puts it, "no greater love has a person than this, to lay down his life for his friends" (John 15:13). Jesus' actions in washing his disciples' feet, which takes place a short while before this comment, can be seen as an enacted parable of the depths of love, of selfless service for the good of others. Jesus' point is not to extol the death of a soldier on a battlefield for his comrades, though of course that is worthy of respect. Rather he is talking about his own sacrificial death for his followers, the death that defeats death and gives them the possibility of eternal life, if they put their trust in him.

Praise begins in the morning; the reference to "before the dawn" is a reminder to the devout Sikh to get up while it is still dark to praise the creator. This is a habit of some Christians, but by no means all. It is enshrined within the practices of the monastic tradition, but not necessarily part of the day-to-day routine of all Christians. Yet for me personally the only "proper" way to start the day is with reading my Bible and in prayer.

The line "through deeds we've done we get this garment" is a reference to karma, as the "garment" is the human body. The point is that our past behaviour determines our present reality. Whilst Christians agree that "you reap what you sow"(Galatians 6:7), this is understood as only applying to the present existence, for Christians believe in resurrection rather than reincarnation. And although we probably mean different things by the word, both Sikhs and Christians are forever grateful for the grace of God that has been shown to them personally.

Stanza five:

> He cannot be established, nor can He be made,
> Of Himself He exists, quite free from all stain.
> Through serving Him truly, great honour is found,
> O Nanak, sing praise of the store of all virtue.
> Sing praises and listen, feel love in your heart,
> Let sorrow be banished and joy take its place.
> Through the guru the Word and its wisdom are shown
> Through the guru awareness of immanence.
> The guru is Shiv, he is Vishnu and Brahma

A CHRISTIAN'S REFLECTIONS ON READING JAPJI

> The guru is Parvati, known as the Mother.
> If I knew Him, I still could not say what He's like,
> His description is something that cannot be told.
> O Guru, teach me only this:
> Let me not forget
> The One who gives to all.

Given the gendered language, it is useful to refer to Kaur Singh's translation of the first three lines:

> That One cannot be moulded or made,
> Alone immaculate and self-existent.
> Those who serve receive honours

She translates the final main line as: "Were I to comprehend, I'd still fail to explain" (Kaur Singh 1995, 53).

The stanza begins with reflection on the self-existence of the divine; existing before and outside of time, Waheguru has no need of any others, existing in purity and holiness. This resonates with a Christian understanding, but I wonder whether it connects with the first question of the Westminster Shorter Confession, which states that human beings were created to worship God and enjoy relationship with him always. There certainly is an emphasis on personal communion with truth, something Christians would want to echo. The instruction to sing is one that Paul also makes:

> Do not get drunk with wine, for that is debauchery; but be filled with the Spirit, as you sing psalms and hymns and spiritual songs among yourselves, singing and making melody to the Lord in your hearts, giving thanks to God the Father at all times and for everything in the name of our Lord Jesus Christ. (Ephesians 5:18-20, NRSV).

Stanza six

Singing strengthens faith, especially when conducted corporately. There is something uplifting and unifying about a gathered congregation singing praise together. I cannot sing very well but I am still uplifted and strengthened in my faith through congregational singing. Although *Japji* is recited by Sikhs alone in the morning, doubtless it is also sung in gurdwaras, where it would have a similar impact of enlivening and enriching faith.

The final part of the stanza appears to be a critique of idol worship. This point is one that runs throughout both the Hebrew Scriptures and also the New Testament. I love in particular the critique in Isaiah of the man who makes an idol from half a tree, and then chops up the other half for firewood. He worships that which he has made from the same material he uses to warm himself at the fireside (Isaiah 40:18-20; 44:9-20). Worship of an idol you yourself have made is thus regarded as a thoroughly futile exercise.

Stanza six:

> His pleasure is my pilgrimage,
> What use is bathing otherwise?
> One lesson from the guru fills
> The mind that hears with precious gems.
> O guru, teach me only this:
> Let me not forget
> The One who gives to all.

The reference to the importance of pilgrimage indicates especially a journey to bathe in a sacred river. The point is thus a physical journey is of little lasting spiritual value if it is not done in the right frame of mind, with the right focus on the divine. Hence the refrain, a prayer that remembrance of the divine remains uppermost in the mind. Pilgrimage is something that Christians do not especially address, because there is no compulsion to pilgrimage in the way there is in Islam for example. Those Christians in the more sacramentally focused traditions do make pilgrimage to particular holy sites (for example the shrine at Walsingham). And it could be argued that the habit of going to a particular Christian conference each year is a form of pilgrimage. But the main point I take from this stanza is questions. Am I in a habit of making holy journeys? How conscious of God am I when I travel? Do I see the divine at work around me as I go?

Stanza seven:

> If one could live for all four ages,
> Or even ten times longer still,
> If one were known in all nine realms,
> Enjoying universal admiration,
> If one acquired great reputation,
> Great fame and glory in the world –
> Yet who would pay the slightest notice,
> Without that look of favour from Him?
> To worms that wretch would be a worm,
> Whom even sinners would condemn.
> To those who lack and those who have them,
> O Nanak, virtues come from Him.
> On Him, though, virtue cannot be
> Conferred by anyone that's here.

The message of this stanza is that true success is a gift of grace. However long one lives, wherever one is active, whatever achievements one can list, ultimately one glance of the guru is enough to bestow favour on the disciple. As Kaur Singh translates,

> If we were to win good name, glory and fame throughout the world,
> But were denied the loving Gaze, we would be cast out,
> Treated as the lowest of worms, accused as criminals (1995, 54).

Stanza seven

There is a verse in the Song of Songs which resonates this idea. The bridegroom describes the bride as follows:

> You have ravished my heart, my sister, my bride,
>   you have ravished my heart with a glance of
>   your eyes,
>   with one jewel of your necklace.
> (Song of Songs 4:9, NRSV).

In some Christian interpretations of this text, this would be Jesus talking to his bride, the Church. The obviously reverses the order of the stanza from *Japji*, where the glance is from the guru (who represents God) towards the disciple. But the point of a gaze of love is the same; all love should be mutual.

Christians also struggle with what it means to be "successful," and invariably conclude that it is better to think in terms of "faithfulness" to the call that God has placed on their lives. Many of the Hebrew prophets were not successful in the conventional sense; their warnings were often ignored. But they are successful in that their messages were preserved for posterity as a warning, and also that they still speak to people today. In the New Testament, Paul writes to the Philippians that for him "to live is Christ, and dying is gain" (Philippians 1:21). His point is that while he is alive, he will serve his Lord, but once he dies, he gets to spend eternity with Christ, so both life and death are equally good in their own way.

As I wrestle with what it means to be employed and active within the church and the world, this is an important reminder that success in the eyes of the world is a very different thing from success in the eyes of God. I think this section makes a similar argument, that it is only by the gift of God that one achieves material or other forms of human success, and it is only as we live out this gift that we grow in our relationship with the divine.

A CHRISTIAN'S REFLECTIONS ON READING JAPJI

Stanzas eight to eleven:

> Through hearing It: the Siddhs and Pirs and sages.
> Through hearing It: the earth and bull and heaven.
> Through hearing It: the zones and worlds and underworlds.
> Through hearing It: death has no power to menace.
> Nanak, the saints gain bliss forever,
> Through hearing It: the end of pain and sin.
>
> Through hearing It: Isar, Brahma, Indra.
> Through hearing It: wicked mouths are filled with praise.
> Through hearing It: yoga and the body's secrets.
>
> Through hearing It: Shastras, Smritis, Vedas.
> Nanak, the saints gain bliss forever,
> Through hearing It: the end of pain and sin.
>
> Through hearing It: truth, contentment, wisdom.
> Through hearing It: bathing in all sixty-eight.
> Through hearing It: reconciliation brings great honour.
> Through hearing It: attention comes quite easily.
> Nanak, the saints gain bliss forever,
> Through hearing It: the end of pain and sin.
>
> Through hearing It: the pool of virtues' depths.
> Through hearing It: the Shaykhs, the Pirs, the kings.
> Through hearing It: the blind can find their way.

Stanzas eight to eleven

> Through hearing It: the bottomless pit is plumbed.
> Nanak, the saints gain bliss forever,
> Through hearing It: the end of pain and sin.

Shackle and Mandair note that "through hearing It" indicates "by listening to the Name." Most lines in this section begin with *suniai*, "through hearing" and then a sequence of nouns which indicate how consciousness is expanded, setting out a "wonderful sense of infinite possibilities" that is sadly lost in translation (2005, 145). The encouragement is that attentive listening, with a quiet and open mind to divine truth, is to be practised even if what is heard is in fact unattractive. The point is that one must quieten the chatter of one's own mind, one's own ego and make space for the divine voice.

The Christian must listen for the "still small voice" of God. This phrase comes from the story of Elijah on Mount Carmel, in his exhaustion and despair finding the presence of God not in the fire or the earthquake, but in the gentle whisper. That whisper was God speaking restoration and hope to one who was exhausted and drained by ministry (1 Kings 19). The lesson of direct provision and protection is one Christians can take from Elijah's period of rest and recuperation.

I think the point argued for in *Japji* is that one must listen for the goodness of God in the midst of one's devotions, and it is only those who have truly learned to quieten their own minds who hear what it is that God has to offer. Thus Kaur Singh's translation uses the refrain "Hearing the Word" (1995, 55). Shackle and Mandair explain the reference to "all sixty-eight" in stanza ten refers to the sixty-eight pilgrimage sites where bathing is considered "especially meritorious" (2005, 145).

There is resonance with the warnings to Christians that they can be so busy rushing around the place that they do

A CHRISTIAN'S REFLECTIONS ON READING JAPJI

not have any sense of what it is that God is actually saying to them or calling them to do. This speaks to me; there is a warning of the danger of being too busy reacting to the urgent to make time to think about what is important. Arguably this is the point that Jesus makes to the sisters Mary and Martha. Jesus visits them in their home, and while Martha busies herself providing food for the assembled gathering, Mary just sits at Jesus' feet. When Martha complains to Jesus about her sister, Jesus responds that Martha is troubled and distract, but Mary has made a good choice, which will not be taken from her (Luke 10:38-42), reminding us that taking time to sit and relate to the divine is of supreme importance.

Stanzas twelve to fifteen:

> The state of acceptance is not to be told,
> If anyone tries, they will later repent.
> With pen on the paper, no hard-thinking writer
> Can capture the slightest idea of acceptance.
> Such is the Name which is free from all stain,
> To be known to the mind through acceptance.

> Through acceptance, awareness envelops the mind.
> Through acceptance, the universe comes to be known.
> Through acceptance, all slaps on the face are avoided.
> Through acceptance, there is no departure with death.
> Such is the Name which is free from all stain,
> To be known to the mind through acceptance.

> Through acceptance, no obstacle stands in our way.
> Through acceptance, we're given distinction and honour.

> Through acceptance, we keep to the road we should travel.
> Through acceptance, right action stays closely connected.
> Such is the Name which is free from all stain,
> To be known to the mind through acceptance.
>
> Through acceptance, we come to discover the gate of salvation.
> Through acceptance, support is provided to us and our kinsfolk.
> Through acceptance, the guru is saved, and he saves his disciples.
> Through acceptance, O Nanak, none need to keep begging.
> Such is the Name which is free from all stain,
> To be known to the mind through acceptance.

Shackle and Mandair explain there is no easy English translation for *manne ki* and its cognate term *mannai*, but argue it indicates a "sense of reverent mindfulness and remembrance" which they suggest is captured by "acceptance" rather than "belief," as the latter indicates an overly rational approach (2005, 145-46). Kaur Singh uses "remembering" (1995, 55-56). Sikhs are therefore encouraged to display complete absorption or immersion on the *shabad*, the divine word. The point is that mental alertness and consciousness should be focused primarily on the divine.

In his letter to the Colossians, Paul urges his audience:

> So, if you have been raised with Christ, seek the things that are above, where Christ is, seated at the right hand of God. Set your minds on things that are above, not on things that are on earth, for you have died, and your life is hidden with Christ in God. (Colossians 3:1-3 NRSV).

A CHRISTIAN'S REFLECTIONS ON READING JAPJI

His focus soon turns practical, explaining that Christians must make active steps to remove "anger, wrath, malice, slander, and abusive language from your mouth" (Colossians 3:8) and instead clothe themselves "with compassion, kindness, humility, meekness, and patience" and focus especially on forgiving others as they themselves have been forgiven, binding all things in place with love that echoes the love Christ has shown to his followers (Colossians 3:12-14). Doubtless the injunction within *Japji* is not just to cerebral contemplation and detachment, but also hints at the need to be active in service of others as a means of demonstrating acceptance and commitment to the will of God.

Stanza sixteen:

> The saints are approved, the saints are supreme,
> The saints receive honour, as they stand in the court.
> The saints are exalted, as kings at the gate,
> The saints' thoughts are fixed on the guru alone.
> Although one may speak and try to describe them,
> The works of the Maker cannot be counted.
> The Bull that is righteousness, offspring of mercy,
> Is tethered in place with the rope of contentment.
> If we can see this, we indeed must acknowledge
> What the burden must be which lies on the bull.
> There are many more worlds beyond earth, then yet more,
> What strength must the one who's beneath them possess?
> The names of the creatures, their kinds and their colours,
> Are all written down by the flow of His pen.

Stanza sixteen

> Suppose that someone knew how to record them,
> How long an account would then have to be written!
> How great is His power, how lovely His beauty!
> How great is His bounty, which cannot be priced!
> With a single command this vast world was created,
> On which hundreds and thousands of currents emerged.
> To describe You is beyond me,
> Your quite unworthy offering.
> That deed is good which pleases You,
> O Formless One, secure forever.

In the New Testament, "the saints" is a reference to all those who have faith in Jesus; later tradition in some expressions of Christianity singles out particularly holy people for beatification as saints, a process that normally requires the individual to have performed at least one attested miracle. It is interesting to think which reference is being made here: is it to all people or to particularly holy followers? Kaur Singh's use of "the chosen" suggests the latter alternative; her translation of the opening line of stanza sixteen is "the chosen win approval, they are the chosen ones." Further on she eschews masculine pronouns to translate "What power and beauty of form. How to estimate the gift" (1995, 56).

The stanza continues by making the point that all that exists is the produce of divine creation. A similar point is made within the Hebrew Scriptures; in the Genesis creation narrative, it is clear that God made the sun, moon and stars, which some cultures believed to be gods and so worshipped. Here, the bull referred to is the mythical bull believed to support the earth, and a similar point is made, that God is creator. Moreover, it is the inner attitude of the heart, righteousness, mercy, contentment that are to be cultivated above all.

A CHRISTIAN'S REFLECTIONS ON READING JAPJI

The focus on creation continues with the reference to the fact that all which exists is written by God. In the Hebrew Scriptures, God speaks creation in to being, but the point is essentially the same; creation occurs at the divine Word, in all its manifest and various forms. As Creator and Originator of all that exists, God is beyond all speech and description.

Stanzas seventeen to nineteen

> Countless the prayers, and countless the reverence,
> Countless the worship, and countless the penance,
> Countless the scriptures and readers of Vedas,
> Countless the yogis whose minds are detached,
> Countless the saints who think on His virtues,
> Countless the pious, and countless the givers,
> Countless the heroes who boldly faced steel,
> Countless the silent absorbed in devotion.
> To describe You is beyond me,
> Your quite unworthy offering.
> That deed is good which pleases You,
> O Formless One, secure forever.
>
> Countless the fools who are totally blind,
> Countless the thieves who live off their crimes,
> Countless the tyrants who issue commands,
> Countless the cut-throats who murder and kill,
> Countless the sinners who sin till they die,
> Countless the liars who go round in lies,
> Countless the outcastes who eat and speak filth,
> Countless the slanderers burdened by spite.
> The lowly Nanak says: I am
> Your quite unworthy offering.
> That deed is good which pleases You,
> O Formless One, secure forever.

Stanzas seventeen to nineteen

> Countless Your titles, and countless Your places,
> Countless and far beyond reach Your domains.
> Calling them countless increases the burden.
> Through words come the Name, through words come the praises,
> Through words come both wisdom and songs to Your virtues.
> Through words come reciting and writing the Word,
> Through words on the forehead, our fate is described.
> The Writer has no words upon Him,
> As He commands, so they receive.
> His Name is great, as is creation.
> There is no place without the Name.
> To describe You is beyond me,
> Your quite unworthy offering.
> That deed is good which pleases You,
> O Formless One, secure forever.

The focus of these three stanzas appears to be the complete range of human activity, everything that people do, both good and bad. Stanza seventeen lists the good actions, stanza eighteen the bad, and then this is contrasted with the reality of the divine, who is far above the good and evil found within creation.

The main question I want to ask of this section is whether good and evil are seen as balanced and in competition, or whether good is presumed to be greater than evil. The Christian notion of evil as the absence of good, and therefore not an entity in its own right, but rather a lack, a non-being, an absence, is one worth exploring in more detail. In Christian thought, evil is real, but by no means equal to God who is pure goodness. Moreover, evil has been defeated at the Cross and death is defeated; as Paul writes to the church in Corinth, death has been swallowed up in victory and no longer has any sting (1 Corinthians 15:54-55).

The worldview that flows from the understanding of good and evil as equal is very different from the worldview that presumes good has triumphed over evil. I am not sure what is being taught here, so do not want to make any presumptions. Rather I note this is an important point for dialogue and discussion. Do we see evil as ultimately defeated, or as having the possibility of triumphing in the end?

What is clear in these three stanzas is that the divine is beyond description. Whilst we may hope to put into words a partial explanation of what God is like, the reality is that we cannot get very close. What we can do is serve, and that is Guru Nanak's response; he recognises that any attempt at service is unworthy, but nevertheless, that if a deed is pleasing in God's sight it is an acceptable offering. Isaiah the Prophet says:

> We have all become like one who is unclean,
>> and all our righteous deeds are like a filthy cloth.
>
> We all fade like a leaf,
>> and our iniquities, like the wind, take us away.
>
> There is no one who calls on your name,
>> or attempts to take hold of you;
>
> for you have hidden your face from us,
>> and have delivered us into the hand of our iniquity.
>
> Yet, O Lord, you are our Father;
>> we are the clay, and you are our potter;
>> we are all the work of your hand. (Isaiah 64:6-8 NRSV).

The tone is slightly different from the stanzas of *Japji* cited above, but there are resonances, in the idea that human striving is insufficient, recognising that when we try to

Stanza twenty

attain the divine in our own strength we fail, but that ultimately, we are made by God to love and serve him, and he will, if he so choses, draw us to himself.

Stanza twenty:

> When dust falls on our limbs and bodies
> It can be washed away with water.
> When urine makes a garment foul
> It can be washed away with soap.
> The colour of the Name will clean
> The mind that is befouled by sins.
> The record of your deeds goes with you,
> 'Saint' and 'sinner' aren't just names.
> It's you who sow, and you who reap,
> O Nanak, birth and death are as decreed.

This develops the idea cited above, that we can cleanse ourselves from physical impurities, of dirt, and urine, but it is only God's Name, his holy Word that can deal with the impurity of the mind. Two New Testament texts spring to mind. First, Jesus is in conflict with a group of Pharisees, who ask for an explanation as to why Jesus and his disciples are not following ritual purity requirements, washing their hands before eating and so forth. Jesus challenges this understanding of purity, and afterwards privately explains to his disciples:

> Do you not see that whatever goes into a person from outside cannot defile, since it enters, not the heart but the stomach, and goes out into the sewer?' (Thus he declared all foods clean.) And he said, 'It is what comes out of a person that defiles. For it is from within, from the human heart, that evil intentions come: fornication, theft, murder, adultery, avarice, wickedness, deceit, licentiousness, envy, slander, pride,

folly. All these evil things come from within, and they defile a person. (Mark 7:18-23, NRSV).

This is not to do away with the requirements of basic hygiene, but rather to point to a person's inner attitude, their state of mind and disposition of their heart as the main causes of impurity and a decision to turn away from God. Jesus is specifically addressing a group perceived to be religious hypocrites. Those who claim to be godly, but whose inner attitude is still sinful are warned of the danger of this position.

The second text comes in Paul's letter to the Galatians, where he writes:

> Do not be deceived; God is not mocked, for you reap whatever you sow. If you sow to your own flesh, you will reap corruption from the flesh; but if you sow to the Spirit, you will reap eternal life from the Spirit. So let us not grow weary in doing what is right, for we will reap at harvest time, if we do not give up. So then, whenever we have an opportunity, let us work for the good of all, and especially for those of the family of faith. (Galatians 6:7-10, NRSV).

The opening observation that God cannot be mocked is an important additional point; those who do evil presume they will get away with it, that their lives can mock and ignore divine standards. The reality is that this is not the case; there will be a judgement, a reckoning, and we will all be accountable for how we have lived. That is Paul's point; it is not enough to declare one has faith. That faith must be lived out through our actions. As stanza 20 of *Japji* puts it, the record of our deeds is known and goes before us. This is a similar point that Paul makes; if we live according to our

Stanza twenty-one

own sinful desires("the flesh") then we will reap the rewards of self-centredness and introspection. But if we strive to live as guided by God's Spirit, desiring his plans, then we will remain in relationship with God for eternity. Paul is particularly keen that followers of Jesus devote time and energy to others who share their faith; in time the Christian ethic of service became more outward focused, but initially at least, it has a particular focus on fellow believers.

Stanza twenty-one:

> Hardly the tiniest grain's worth of honour
> Comes through bathing, austerity, pity and charity.
> Hearing, acceptance, love in the heart
> Show the place for true bathing and cleansing within.
> All virtues are Yours, in me there are none.
> Without practising virtue, there is no devotion
> I salute You, Creator, the World and the Word,
> The True and the Lovely, delight of my heart!
> What was the time, what was the hour?
> What was the date by moon and by sun?
> What was the month, what was the season?
> When did the world come into being?
> The time was not found by the Pandits,
> For it to be in the Puranas.
> The hour was not found by the Qazis,
> For the Koran to record it.
> The date is unknown to the yogis,
> None know the season or month.
> The One who created this world,
> The Creator alone knows the time.
> How can I speak, how can I praise?
> How can I tell, how can I know?
> Plenty pretend they can tell,
> Nanak, they claim to be smart.

A CHRISTIAN'S REFLECTIONS ON READING JAPJI

> Great is the Lord great is His Name
> Whatever He does come to pass.

This stanza repeats the teaching of the indescribable and unreachable nature of the divine, far above all human comprehension and effort. However hard we strive to be pure; we have no hope of attaining unity with the divine in our own strength. The focus of the text shifts to creation, which is outside of human control or effort. Whilst religious teachers may set themselves up as having great authority, *Japji* reminds us that these people did not create or orginate anything, everything comes from Waheguru. The proper response to this is to demonstrate humility, recognising one's own limited nature. It is striking that Kaur Singh's translation concludes with

> Great is the Sovereign, great is Its Name, all that happens is Its doing,
> Says Nanak, but those who claim credit stay unadorned in the hearafter (1995, 59).

The use of "It" illustrates the challenge of finding appropriate pronouns when you wish to be clear the divine is not bound by human constructs of gender. But the text also makes clear the indescribable nature of *Akal Purakh*: "You are Truth, You are Beauty, You are Joy Eternal" (1995, 59).

A similar thought about the limited nature of humanity in contrast to the divine is expressed in Psalm 8, which talks about the lowly place of humanity when viewed with the proper perspective of God's creation.

> When I look at your heavens, the work of your fingers,
> the moon and the stars that you have established;

Stanza twenty-two

> what are human beings that you are mindful of
> them,
> > mortals that you care for them? (Psalm 8:3-4, NRSV).

The Psalm goes on to celebrate the status of humanity, and the responsibility that people have to care for creation. But it closes with praise of the Lord. This is the right response to any discussion of God, who is worthy of all our worship and adoration.

Stanza twenty-two:

> Lower worlds below each other,
> Heavens thousand fold above:
> That search for limits is exhausting
> Is the Vedas' sole conclusion.
> All Puranas and the scriptures
> Agree there is one basic source.
> It would be written if they could,
> But it can't be written down.
> Nanak, simply call Him great,
> It's He who knows how great He is.

This stanza turns the focus towards the divine, and how much greater the Creator is than the created. The particular focus is on how scripture is inadequate to describe God. In his conclusion to his Gospel, John writes:

> there are also many other things that Jesus did; if every one of them were written down, I suppose that the world itself could not contain the books that would be written. (John 21:25, NRSV)

A CHRISTIAN'S REFLECTIONS ON READING JAPJI

This is hyperbole, just as in *Japji* above. The point is that however hard humans strive, even the best poetry, the greatest of hymns or songs, only give us a glimpse of the divine. I was challenged through reading a book by J B Phillips entitled *Your God is Too Small*, which made the point repeatedly that human conceptions of the divine are limited and flawed. The Apostle Paul puts it this way:

> For now we see in a mirror, dimly, but then we will see face to face. Now I know only in part; then I will know fully, even as I have been fully known. (1 Corinthians 13:12, NRSV)

The point is that any reflection in a mirror is only a partial, two-dimensional representation. It is therefore incomplete and inadequate. In the same way, Paul suggests, we have only limited knowledge of God. For Paul, full knowledge will come at the resurrection of the dead, when we see God face to face. For Guru Nanak, that full knowledge comes through absorption into the divine.

Stanzas twenty-three to twenty-six record the infinity of the divine in contrast with humanity's puny finite existence. They are discussed together:

> The praises which praisers express
> Do not gain them sufficient awareness.
> Once rivers and channels flow into the sea
> They no longer remain distinct.
> Rulers and kings may possess
> Oceans and mountains of wealth,
> But are less than the tiniest ant
> In whose mind He is never forgotten.

Stanzas twenty-three to twenty-six

There's no end to His praise, no end to its telling,
There's no end to His works, no end to His giving.
There's no end to His seeing, no end to His hearing,
There's no end that is known to what's in His mind.
There's no end that is known to the world that He made,
There's no end that is known to His limits.
Though many may yearn to determine them,
His boundaries cannot be found.
None can discover this limit,
Which always exceeds its description.
Great is the Lord, and high is His place
And higher than high is His Name.
Only if we were as high as He is
Could we hope to determine His height.
Only to Him can His greatness be known,
Nanak, the glance of His grace is our gift.

Great is His kindness, which cannot be written,
Great is the Giver, who has no grain of greed.
So many, the crowds of the heroes who beg,
So many, their numbers cannot be reckoned.
So many are wasted and ruin their gifts,
So many keep getting, but deny they've received.

So many are fools who just keep on consuming,
So many keep suffering sorrow and hunger.
These also are gifts which You give us.
Your will determines release from our bondage,
No one else has a say about this.
Any loud-mouth who speaks up should know
He'll be shamed and his face will be slapped.
The Knower and Giver are one and the same,
Though this is acknowledged by few.

A CHRISTIAN'S REFLECTIONS ON READING JAPJI

> Those granted the gift of offering praise,
> Nanak says, will be kings over kings.
>
> Priceless Your virtues, priceless Your dealings,
> Priceless Your traders, priceless Your treasures,
> Priceless Your commers, priceless Your buyers,
> Priceless Your lovers, priceless Your mergers,
> Priceless Your justice, priceless Your court,
> Priceless Your balance, priceless Your weights,
> Priceless Your bounty, priceless Your seal,
> Priceless Your mercy, priceless Your order.
> Priceless, so priceless, You cannot be told,
> Though the effort absorbs us in love.
> The Vedas, Puranas and scriptures all tell,
> The commentaries and the great scholars all tell,
>
> The Brahmas all tell, the Govindas tell too,
> The Isars all tell, and so too do the Siddhs,
> The numbers created of Buddhas all tell,
> The demons all tell, and so too do the gods,
> The sages all tell, and so too do the yogis.
> So many are telling and trying to tell,
> So many while telling rise up and depart.
> You could make many more than all these,
> He's as great as He chooses to be,
> As is known to the True One Himself.
> Any loud-mouth who dares to describe Him,
> Should be branded 'most stupid of fools'.

In this long section, the point is made, again and again, that the divine is without limits, that divine mercy, grace, gifts, goodness are all without end. Any and all possible beings, both human, animal, and spiritual, all recognise that the divine is greater and cannot be adequately described. There are many texts in the Hebrew Scriptures and the New Testament which make this same point, including the hymn

Stanza twenty-seven

to Wisdom in Proverbs 8, the rebuke of Job by God in Job 38-41, and the descriptions of Jesus in Philippians 2 and Colossians 1. All our attempts to describe God are simply too small and limited.

Returning to the point about gendered language, Kaur-Singh's translation of stanza twenty-four begins:

> Infinite is Your glory, and infinite the ways to sing Your praise,
> Infinite are the deeds, and infinite the gifts,
> Infinite is the seeing, and infinite the hearing
> And infinite are the workings of That Mind.
> Infinite is the variety of forms,
> Infinite are the edges of the universe (1995, 60).

Stanza twenty-seven:

> How great is that gate, and how great is that house,
> Where You sit and take care of all things!
> So many instruments, so many players,
> So many ragas and so many singers!
> To You sing the wind and the water and fire,
> To You sings the Judge at the gate,
> To You sing the writers called Chitra and Gupta,
> Whose record assists the Judge to decide.
> To You sing too Isar and Brahma, adorned
> In their glory along with the goddess.
> To You sing too Indras enthroned on their seats
> Along with the gods at the gate.
> To You sing the Siddhs in profound meditation,
> To You sing the saints in their deep contemplation.
> To You sing the true, the content and the celibate,

A CHRISTIAN'S REFLECTIONS ON READING JAPJI

> To You sing the warriors, the fiercest of heroes,
> To You sing the pandits and greatest of rishis,
> Reciting the Vedas throughout all the ages,
> To You sing the fair ones who capture the heart
> In heaven, on earth, and down in the underworld.
> To You sing the jewels which You have created
> Along with the sixty-eight places of bathing.
> To You sing the fighters whose strength is heroic,
> To You sing the quadruple orders of being.
> To You sing the realms and the spheres and the worlds,
> Which You created and You have preserved.
> To You sing all those in whom You delight,
> The saints who are steeped in the joy of Your love.
> To You sing so many I cannot remember,
> Says Nanak, how can I conceive them?
> It is He, it is He who always is True
> The Lord who is True, and True is His Name.
> He is and He will be, never departing,
> The One who created the whole of creation.
> He fashioned the spectacle this world presents
> In its multiple colours and various kinds.
> He makes and He watches what He has created
> As fully accords with His infinite greatness.
> He always will act in the way that He pleases,
> No order can ever be issued to rule Him.
> It is He who is sovereign, the king of all kings,
> Nanak says, to whose pleasure all life must be subject.

Shackle and Mandair note that this stanza, known as *Sodar* from its opening words *so dar*, "that gate," is also prescribed for recitation in the evening service called *Sodar*

Stanzas twenty-eight to thirty-one

Rahiras. They add that "the Judge" referred to in the sixth line is *Dharamraj*, who judges the souls after death, and that the "quadruple orders of being" are the four sources of life, which can be created from wombs, eggs, plants and sweat (2005, 146).

This stanza is a hymn of praise to Waheguru's infinite greatness. There are echoes of some of the Psalms, and their praise of God, for example in Psalm 150. Yet the tone is also somehow qualitatively different. I think it is perhaps the gathering in of other faith traditions within *Japji* that you do not find in the Psalms. The Hebrew Scriptures do clearly appropriate and use the thoughts and texts of other religious perspectives.[1] But they are subsumed into a fundamentally Jewish worldview, in a way that is not present in *Japji*. That seems to allow Muslims and Hindus to be themselves, although that must stand in tension with Nanak's observation that there is no Hindu and no Muslim.

Stanzas twenty-eight to thirty-one are united by a common refrain, and will be considered together:

> Let contentment be your earrings, modesty your pouch
> Let meditation be the ashes smeared upon you.
> With fear of death as cloak to wrap your virgin body
> Make faith your yoga, let it be the staff you wield.
> With all humanity belonging to your order
> Let conquest of the mind bring conquest of the world.
> All hail, all hail to Him,
> The primal, untouched, unstarted, unchanging,
> Throughout all the ages the same!

---

1. An additional observation is that Christians have appropriated the Hebrew Scriptures and re-interpreted them utilising a Christological framework that presumes Jesus of Nazareth is the Messiah.

A CHRISTIAN'S REFLECTIONS ON READING JAPJI

> The food of wisdom is dispensed by mercy,
> The mystic music sounds in every heart.
> God is the lord who has complete control,
> Beyond all riches and all magic powers.
> Union and separation work in rhythm,
> And all receive the fortune which is written.
> All hail, all hail to Him,
> The primal, untouched, unstarted, unchanging,
> Throughout all the ages the same!
>
> One the mother, made according to design,
> Three the disciples who meet with acceptance:
> Creator, provider, and holder of court,
> Each set to work as He commands and wills,
> Who sees, unseen, how wonderful this is!
> All hail, all hail to Him,
> The primal, untouched, unstarted, unchanging,
> Throughout all the ages the same!
>
> His seat and His stores are in every world,
> Whatever is found there was placed all at once.
> The Creator first made, and then He beholds,
> Nanak, the works of the True One are true.
> All hail, all hail unto Him,
> The primal, untouched, unstarted, unchanging,
> Throughout all the ages the same!

The focus here is on how to live. The seeker after the divine is encouraged to cultivate contentment, modesty, chastity, self-discipline, a catholic and universal outlook, one focused on service, knowledge and compassion. Rather than seek outward adornment, the believer decorates her or himself with good character, which is infinitely more attractive. As Peter writes in his first letter,

> Do not adorn yourselves outwardly by braiding your hair, and by wearing gold ornaments or

fine clothing; rather, let your adornment be the
inner self with the lasting beauty of a gentle and
quiet spirit, which is very precious in God's sight.
(1 Peter 3:3-4, NRSV).

Wives are the focus of Peter's instruction, but there is no reason to limit the application to this particular group. Rather there is an injunction towards everyone to be more concerned with the attitudes of one's heart, not outward appearance, which is after all the criteria God uses for judging people (1 Samuel 16:7).

The implication of these stanzas is that the main focus of one's life should be spiritual things, rather than material ones. When Jesus' disciples urge him to eat, he replies that his food is to do the work of the one who sent him (John 4:34). The focus is primarily on spiritual living, on pleasing God in how we behave, in particular by renouncing all attachment to the world. There are Christian understandings that focus on renunciation of the world; yet at the same time there is a strong and vital strand within Christian thinking that celebrates all that exists in the world; Jesus providing an abundant supply of wine at the wedding in Cana is a case in point (John 2). You cannot accuse Jesus of being a kill joy aesthetic – indeed he is accused of being a glutton and a drunkard for eating with tax collectors and those deemed sinful (Matthew 11:19; Luke 7:34). This raises really interesting questions about what constitutes life in all its fullness. What does it mean to be fully devoted to God, to be in the world and yet not of it? Walking that tightrope is a continual challenge for all people of faith.

Stanza thirty-two:

> If this one tongue became a hundred thousand,
> If they in turn were multiplied by twenty,
> They would take a hundred thousand times

A CHRISTIAN'S REFLECTIONS ON READING JAPJI

> To praise the one Name of the Lord.
> This is the way to climb the stairs
> That lead to union with Him.
> By hearing such accounts of heaven
> The humblest worms are roused to act.
> Through grace alone is He attained,
> Not through those liars' idle boasts.

Stanza thirty-two returns to a theme already raised in *Japji*, namely that it is impossible for human beings to adequately describe or praise the divine. This is an important reminder of the all-too-human tendency to limit and confine God to a place where we are comfortable; to even attempt to re-create the divine either in our own image, or in an image which we are sure we can master. But the repeated refrain of *Japji*, as indeed of Christian faith, is that it is only by the grace of God we can be enter into any form of relationship with the divine. Whilst we might want to think we have merit of our own, the reality is that we are utterly dependent on divine providence. But this is not a terrifying prospect, rather it is freedom and comforting, because it means we do not need to worry about our own image or status, but concentrate instead on worship and enjoyment of relationship with the one who made us and loves us.

Stanza thirty-three:

> Saying and silence are not in our power,
> Begging and giving are not in our power,
> Living and dying are not in our power.
> The gaining of riches and empire, which causes
> Such mental distraction, is not in our power.
> True awareness and wisdom are not in our power,
> Escape from the world is not in our power.
> Power rests with the One who makes and who watches –

Stanza thirty-three

> Nanak, the high and the low are as nothing before Him.

This stanza develops the thought of the previous one, reminding us of our utter powerlessness and hopelessness. It makes me think of Job's response after being confronted by the Lord:

> 'I know that you can do all things,
> and that no purpose of yours can be thwarted.
> "Who is this that hides counsel without knowledge?"
> Therefore I have uttered what I did not understand,
> things too wonderful for me, which I did not know.
> "Hear, and I will speak;
> I will question you, and you declare to me."
> I had heard of you by the hearing of the ear,
> but now my eye sees you;
> therefore I despise myself,
> and repent in dust and ashes.' (Job 42:2-6, NRSV).

The Lord has been speaking to Job, reminding him of all the things that Job does not understand or cannot control. And Job, who for much of the text has been complaining about God and demanding an audience with and vindication from God now, in all humility, recognises his own limitations and weakness and so repents. It is a continual human weakness to presume we are greater or more important than we actually are. Daily recitation of sentiments such as those in this stanza of *Japji* strike me as an excellent prophylactic, to keep the ego suitably constrained.

A CHRISTIAN'S REFLECTIONS ON READING JAPJI

Stanza thirty-four:

> Nights, seasons, weekdays, lunar dates,
> Winds, water, fire and lower worlds,
> And in the midst of these lies earth,
> Fixed as the place of righteous action,
> Containing different kinds of creatures,
> Whose names are many and untold.
> They are judged according to their deeds,
> As He is true, so is His court.
> Approved, the saints are glorified,
> For they receive His mark of grace.
> There bad and good will stand revealed,
> On going there, this will be known.

Stanza thirty-four explains that we are located in Dharam Khand, in the world of time, space and mind, we must become aware of the order of which we are part, which in the Sikh cosmology includes four other realms of action, as noted above. Discussion of that issue need not distract us from the focus here, which is on the fact that people are accountable for their deeds. Within Sikhi that accountability is experienced through karma, whereby the actions of this life impact on the nature of one's rebirth, or the possibility of escaping from the cycle of birth and re-birth by attaining union with the divine.

Christians, by contrast, do not understand time to be cyclical but linear, and therefore teach that people will die once, and after that face judgement (Hebrews 9:27). Jesus teaches about the nature of that judgement, and makes it clear verbal profession of faith is insufficient; that faith must be evidenced in righteous action responding to the needs of others, perhaps particularly fellow Christians, but certainly not exclusively them. Jesus speaks of judgement at the end of time when he will separate all people as sheep

Stanzas thirty-five and thirty-six

are separated from goats. The means of division is not faith but action; those who have cared for the sick, fed the hungry, clothed the naked, visited the prisoner are held to be righteous, for by doing so they have served Christ (Matthew 25:31-48).

Stanzas thirty-five and thirty-six:

> Such is the realm of righteous action,
> Now to describe the realm of wisdom:
> So many winds and fires and waters,
> So many Krishnas and Maheshes,
> So many Brahmas are created,
> Of varied shapes and forms and colours!
> So many peaks and earths to act in,
> So many Dhruvs to give instruction,
> So many Indras, moons and suns,
> So many spheres there are and countries!
> So many Buddhas, Siddhs and Naths,
> So many goddesses incarnate,
> So many demons, gods and sages,
> So many jewel-bearing oceans!
> So many kinds of life and language,
> So many emperors and kings,
> So many mystics and attendants!
> O Nanak, there' no end, no end.

> In that realm, wisdom reigns supreme
> With music, song, delight and joy.
> The realm of bliss is forged so finely
> That beauty is its only language.
> It cannot be described at all,
> Whoever tries must soon repent.
> Forged here are wisdom and perception,
> The insights of the Siddhs and sages.

The focus shifts from action to the realm of wisdom. There is an interlude in the book of Job where there is a hymn to Wisdom, which begins by discussing mining, noting that whilst men may dig for coal, copper, silver, gold and diamonds, they are unable to mine for wisdom. Indeed people do not know where to find wisdom; it is only found in God:

> God understands the way to it,
>   and he knows its place.
> For he looks to the ends of the earth,
>   and sees everything under the heavens.
> When he gave to the wind its weight,
>   and apportioned out the waters by measure;
> when he made a decree for the rain,
>   and a way for the thunderbolt;
> then he saw it and declared it;
>   he established it, and searched it out.
> And he said to humankind,
> "Truly, the fear of the Lord, that is wisdom;
>   and to depart from evil is understanding."
>   (Job 28:23-28, NRSV).

Within all creation, wisdom only comes from God, who created the world in and through wisdom. In Proverbs chapter eight, Wisdom speaks, informing all who will listen that she offers intelligence, nobility, and truth. She is distant from ignorance, base behaviour and lies. Wisdom teaches that righteousness comes through fear of the Lord, and that she is the one by whom rulers keep their power and dispense justice. Moreover, wisdom was there at creation, the first to be created and the one who rejoiced with God as creation came into being. Wisdom is seen as the way to truly live:

> "And now, my children, listen to me:
>   happy are those who keep my ways.
> Hear instruction and be wise,
>   and do not neglect it.
> Happy is the one who listens to me,

Stanza thirty-seven

> watching daily at my gates,
> waiting beside my doors.
> For whoever finds me finds life
> and obtains favour from the Lord;
> but those who miss me injure themselves;
> all who hate me love death." (Proverbs 8:32-36, NRSV).

So many seek for and try to dispense wisdom, but it can only really be found in God.

Stanza thirty-seven:

> It's power and nothing else which is
> The language of the realm of action.
> Its warriors, those mighty heroes,
> Are strengthened by the force of Ram,
> In glory there are many Sitas,
> Whose beauty cannot be described.
> Those in whose minds Ram's Name resides
> Can neither die nor be deceived.
> There many worlds of saints rejoice
> To have the True One in their hearts.
> The realm of truth is where the Formless
> Resides and, watching all creation
> Makes happy by a look of favour.
> These universes, realms and spheres
> Surpass all efforts to describe them.
> These worlds on worlds and countless forms
> All operate by His command.
> He watches, pleased as He regards them.
> Nanak says: To tell of this is hard as eating iron.

The legend of the god Ram's love for Sita, and his trials and tribulations rescuing her from captivity to Ravana, is part of the epic tale, the Ramayana. The point here is that

A CHRISTIAN'S REFLECTIONS ON READING JAPJI

Ram is known as a warrior of great courage and prowess, and Sita for her extra-ordinary beauty. As a couple they exemplify wholehearted devotion to one another. But all this pales into insignificance compared to the beauty and dedication of those who devote themselves to the praise of the Name, of the divine.

That the divine is incomparable and love is a common refrain in the Psalms. David wrote:

> O God, you are my God, I seek you,
>   my soul thirsts for you;
> my flesh faints for you,
>   as in a dry and weary land where there is no water.
> So I have looked upon you in the sanctuary,
>   beholding your power and glory.
> Because your steadfast love is better than life,
>   my lips will praise you.
> So I will bless you as long as I live;
>   I will lift up my hands and call on your name.
>   (Psalm 63:1-4, NRSV).

Elsewhere, psalms speak of God's commands as the greatest thing in existence, sweeter than honey and more desirable than gold(Psalm 19:10; 119:127). The ordinances of God are all that is necessary for true life.

Stanza thirty-eight:

> With restraint as the furnace, persistence as goldsmith,
> With awareness as anvil, true knowledge as hammer,
> With fear as the bellows, with penance as burner,
> In love as the vessel, the Name is dissolved,

Stanza thirty-eight

> Producing the Word in the mint that is true.
> This is what those who are favoured perform,
> Blessed by His glance of kindness and grace.

The final numbered stanza concludes with a focus on individual spiritual development, on the cultivation of restraint, of the essential nature of patience, discernment and knowledge. The individual disciple is likened to the product of a blacksmith, who is equipped to free the mind from *manmukh*, orientation towards the ego, cast in the mould of love in which the Name is dissolved, producing instead *gurmukh*, one orientated towards the guru. There are echoes here of Paul's injunction to the Philippians to work out their salvation with fear and trembling as God wills and acts within them to his good purposes (Philippians 2:12-13). We must act but we are also powerless; it is only when our actions become fully infused with the divine that they have any lasting value.

The concluding *shalok*:

> Air is the guru and water the father, great earth is the mother,
> Day and night are the nurses who dandle the world.
> In the court Death recites all our deeds, good and bad,
> Which decide who is close, who is far from the Presence.
> Some think on the Name and depart having worked well,
> How bright are their faces, with them how many are freed!

Shackle and Mandair explain that this final *shalok* is generally attributed to the second Guru, Angad, and forms an addition to *Japji* (2005, 146). It is a fitting summary to this great masterpiece of praise and devotional instruction, summarising the essential point, that we are judged according to how we live, and if we chose to live with our consciousness and actions orientated towards the divine, then not only can we make great spiritual progress ourselves, but also can influence the life of others for good. As for Sikhs, so also for Christians; faith is not something that can be practised in isolation, but only in the company of fellow disciples and within the wider world. How can you love your neighbours as yourself if you never meet them?

Chapter 4

The *Janam Sakhis*

The Guru Granth Sahib is primarily hymns and does not contain much detail about Guru Nanak's life. That information is found primarily in the *janam sakhis*. This chapter begins with an introduction to Nanak's life through discussion of the *janam sakhis* before contrasting the views of three scholars: W. H. McLeod, Kirpal Singh and Toby Johnson as to the provenance and purpose of the *janam sakhis*. It concludes with a framework for further discussion of the stories of Guru Nanak and Jesus Christ, which take place in subsequent chapters.

Introducing the Janam Sakhis and Guru Nanak's life

As a simple level, *janam sakhi* can be translated as "birth stories" or "life stories." Anne Murphy (2016, 95) describes the *janam sakhis* as "witnessings of the life" of Guru Nanak, a

THE *JANAM SAKHIS*

useful phrase if "witness" is understood in the sense of "giving testimony" or "explaining what and why I believe." The *janam sakhis* are stories of the Guru's life, told to illustrate a particular point or historical incident within the formative period of the Sikh faith.

Shackle gives a helpful definition of the *janam sakhis*:

> Short individual episodes, called sakhi or 'witness,' typically describe the miraculous powers of the Guru, through which he overcomes his opponents who finally submit to his spiritual authority. These are organized to form very loose narratives, beginning with the Guru's birth and early life, including his professional employment, then describing the start of his mission and his travels within Punjab and beyond, before ending with his establishment of the first Sikh centre at Kartarpur and appointment before his death of Guru Angad as his successor. Many episodes include a hymn said to have been sung by the Guru to the accompaniment of his faithful companion, his Muslim musician Mardana, and quite often it is the content of this hymn which provides the kernel of narrative incident (2016, 115).

The *janam sakhis* are vital for Sikhi; without them, it would be hard to reconstruct the life of the Guru, and without the context of the narrative thread of his life, it would be difficult to understand the radical nature of his message.

Johnson (2015, 33-48) discusses what he describes as the "textual lineages" of the *janam sakhis*. He explains that they began with stories collected by family and friends, as oral traditions which were able to travel further and faster than the Guru himself, presenting his teachings and ideas to those

Introducing the Janam Sakhis and Guru Nanak's life

who were unable to meet him in person. Johnson adds that the extant *janam sakhis* are all dated well after Guru Nanak's death, indicating that they must therefore have been subject to "editorial additions, changes or redactions" (2015, 35).

After the initial phase of the Sikh faith when stories were shared in a primarily *ad hoc* fashion, efforts were made to systematise and organise the accounts. The first of these was arguably Bhai Gurdas' *Var I*. Johnson explains:

> Bhai Gurdas was a nephew of the third Guru, Amar Das (1479-1574), and was close to the next three Gurus as well (Guru Ram Das 1534-1581, Guru Arjan 1563-1606 and Guru Hargobind 1595-1644). Bhai Gurdas was the scribe who assisted Guru Arjan in compiling the Adi Granth in 1604. His Vars (ballads) are a record of the Sikh community and traditions that are unmatched by any other source. They are generally regarded as the "key to the Guru Granth Sahib," as Bhai Gurdas' insights and elaborations on the scriptures were taken as authoritative by the community. Var I is a record, albeit a sparse one, of anecdotes giving a brief outline of Guru Nanak's life in a rough chronology and through accounts of his travels (2015, 36).

The precise provenance of Bhai Gurdas's writings is disputed by scholars: while McLeod rejects the notion of any connection to eyewitness testimony, Kirpal Singh argues that the *Vars I* is based on the recollections of Bhai Buddha (1506-1631), who was a contemporary of Guru Nanak. Whichever of these is true, as Johnson states, a consistent framework of Guru Nanak's life was established by "someone who was close to the lineage of the Gurus and had intimate knowledge of Guru Nanak's verses" (2015, 37).

THE *JANAM SAKHIS*

As Johnson explains, the material that eventually came to be referred to as *janam sakhis* were originally called *janam patris* (birth horoscopes), as they were comparable to the horoscopes produced by Brahmins for their children (2015, 37). But as the tradition developed, it took on a more robust, detailed literary character and told the story of the whole of the Guru's life; hence the change in name. Through the telling and re-telling of the stories, narrative traditions were formed. These include the "popularly personal and fantastic accounts" of the *Bala janam sakhi*, as well as two composite manuscripts now known as the *Puratan* (ancient) *janam sakhi* and the *Adi* (first) *sakhi*. There are also the *Miharban janam sakhi*, linked to the "schismatic Mina sect," the eighteenth century *janam sakhi of Bhat Mani Singh*, which is closely linked to the tenth Guru, Guru Gobind Singh, as well as two manuscripts known by their library catalogue designations, *LDP 194* and *B-40* (Johnson 2015, 38).

Johnson cites McLeod's four stage developmental process of the tradition. First, random collection of material, with no specifical organizational principle at work. Second, organization of the narrative. Third, development of different discourses within the organised text, for example focus on simple narration of Nanak's teaching, or adding in exposition or codes of discipline. The fourth stage was the emergence of print editions of the texts (2015, 38-39).

Before delving further into the detail of the tradition, I will first give an overview of Nanak's life. As Cole and Sambhi explain,

> Guru Nanak was born into a Bedi got of the Khatri zat, a caste whose occupation was commerce and kindred activities. He seems to have been brought up an orthodox Hindu in a district where there were both Hindus and Muslims in the population. His father was revenue superintendent for Rai Bular the Muslim landlord of

> the village of Talwandi. Innumerable stories are
> told in the janam sákhis to show that Nanak, as
> he may be called before he began his ministry,
> was already destined for greatness (2006, 9).

These include the fact that at seven months he would already sit in the posture of a yogi. He rejected the sacred thread ceremony at the age of ten, and thwarted his father's attempts to train him as an accountant. He met with many yogis, sadhus and sants, and although he rejected worldly positions, was doubtless well educated by adulthood.

His older sister Nanaki married Jai Ram, and went to live in the town of Sultanpur, where he was steward to Daulat Khan Lodi. Aged around sixteen, Nanak moved to be with his sister, and also found employment serving Daulat Khan. When he was around nineteen, Nanak married and had two children. The *janam sakhis* record him "as a spiritual preceptor, rising before dawn to bathe in the river and after meditation leading his followers in the singing of kirtan before returning home for breakfast and work in the nawab's offices" (Cole and Sambhi 2006, 10).

One morning Nanak did not return from bathing; it was three days before he was seen again, and when he did reappear, he was silent for a further day, before uttering his enigmatic pronouncement, "there is no Hindu and no Mussulman so whose path shall I follow? I shall follow God's path. God is neither Hindu nor Mussulman and the path which I follow is God's." Nanak explained that

> He was taken to the court of God and escorted
> into the divine presence. There a cup was filled
> with amrit (nectar) and was given to him with
> the command, "This is the cup of the adoration
> of God's name. Drink it. I am with you. I bless
> you and raise you up. Whoever remembers you

THE *JANAM SAKHIS*

> will enjoy my favour. Go, rejoice in my name and
> teach others to do so. I have bestowed the gift
> of my name upon you. Let this be your calling."
> (Cole and Sambhi 2006, 10-11)

Cole and Sambhi add that Nanak's first utterance after this experience was the *mul mantar*, which encapsulates his experience of divinity. Cole and Sambhi quote a passage from the Guru Granth Sahib which also describes the experience, and may be the origin of the *janam sakhi* tradition:

> I was once a worthless minstrel then the Divine One gave me work; I received the primal injunction: Sing divine glory night and day! The sovereign called the minstrel to the True Mansion: I was given the robe of honouring and exalting; I tasted the food of the true ambrosial Name. Those who, through the Guru, feast on the Divine food win eternal joy and peace. Your minstrel spreads your glory by singing your Word. Nanak says, by exalting the Truth we attain the Absolute One (AG 150, cited in Cole and Sambhi 2006, 11).

Cole and Sambhi go on to explain that the *janam sakhis* now proclaim Nanak as Guru, and recall his journeys "to the main centres of Hinduism and Islam as well as to Sri Lanka and Tibet." Many of the narratives focus on Guru Nanak's work in "restoring a religion from the formalism which had overcome it to the truth which lay within it," as well as "describing what true religion is." Cole and Sambhi conclude that Nanak was a mystic in the sense of "a person who, through his experience, perceived an ultimate unity in existence," which he proclaimed to all (2006, 11-13).

As his following increased, aged around fifty, Guru Nanak ceased the travelling that fills much of the *janam sakhis* and settled with his family at Kartarpur, establishing a more settled community, which coalesced into the people that constitute Sikhi today.

Scholarly views on the *janam sakhis* vary considerably, from those who argue they have little or no historical value to those who understand them as essential for re-telling the history of Guru Nanak's life afresh to each generation of the faithful. In what follows, these two views are contrasted before a third way of understanding the *janam sakhis* is proposed.

McLeod on the Janam Sakhis

The first scholar whose views will be discussed is W. H. McLeod, who is a sceptic as to the historical value of the *janam sakhis*. McLeod comments that the Guru Granth Sahib "provides us with surprisingly little information" concerning the actual events of Guru Nanak's life (1968, 7), a point that is indisputable, since the Guru Granth Sahib is not a biography. An alternative source of detail on Guru Nanak's life are the *janam sakhis*, but McLeod finds them equally unsatisfactory, albeit for an entirely different reason, namely that a "very substantial proportion" of the stories are "obviously legend," and moreover, "what cannot be summarily dismissed in this way is open to grave suspicion on other grounds" (1968, 8). McLeod does concede that there is some historical foundation "beneath a superstructure of legend," but he does not have much confidence in the reliability of the *janam sakhis* for detail of Guru Nanak's life (1968, 9).

McLeod could be characterised as an extreme sceptic as to the historicity of the *janam sakhi* material. In his discussion of what is arguably Guru Nanak's signature statement, and a foundational doctrine of Sikhi, namely that "there is neither Hindu nor Mussulman," McLeod comments that "it is quite possible that this aphorism derives from an authentic utterance by Guru Nanak, but the general unreliability of the *janam sakhis* forbids a positive affirmation on this point" (1968, 12). Thus, McLeod does not completely reject the possibility of historical accuracy, but he remains largely unconvinced as to the possibility of historical reconstruction on any meaningful level of detail. If even such a foundational event is regarded with scepticism, what hope is there for other events to be given this status?

As he outlines his reconstruction of the life of Guru Nanak, McLeod also explains his own worldview. For example, McLeod argues that any incident that refers to the "miraculous or the plainly fantastic" must be rejected out of hand, although no reason is given for this unsubstantiated assertion (1968, 68). He adds that "The strict, at times ruthless, approach is as much required in a quest for the historical Nanak as it has been required in the quest of the historical Jesus" (1968, 68). This is a fascinating comment, because it is a position adopted by some, but by no means all, scholars in the quest for the historical Jesus, and many attempts to reconstruct the historical Jesus that have been written subsequent to 1968 have presumed the miraculous is possible (not least N T Wright 1993, 1996, 2003).

McLeod has five categories (established, probable, possible, improbable and impossible) and seven criteria for deciding which category to allocate the different stories to (1968, 68-69). These are:

1. The miraculous, which are rejected out of hand

2. Testimony of external sources

3. Guru Nanak's work as recorded in the Guru Granth Sahib

4. Agreement between different *janam sakhis*

5. The relative reliability of different *janam sakhis*

6. A measure of trust can be attached to the genealogical references

7. Geographic criterion; travels in the Punjab are more likely to be accurate

McLeod begins his survey with those *sakhis* he regards as impossible, and so rejects out of hand, before turning to those that are improbable and possible. He allocates eighty-seven of the total of one hundred and twenty four *sakhis* that he has identified to these three categories, and the majority of those that remain are allocated to "probable," leaving only a few that McLeod regards as established.

Sikh scholars reject McLeod's views

McLeod's views have unsurprisingly engendered a negative backlash from some Sikh scholars, who reject his characterisation of the *janam sakhis* as lacking any historical basis. To give one example, Ahluwalia explains that history "is not a chronicle of events, a narration of happenings, or a compilation of empirical data; it is also not a linear sequencing of occurrences," but should be understood as "a perspectival resurrection of the past" in which the past loses its "pastness" and is experienced as "a living presence" (2001, 73-74). Although Ahluwalia does not name McLeod specifically, he does criticise attempts to "de-historicise" the history of the Punjab in general and Sikhs in particular. Whether Ahluwalia is criticizing a sceptical approach to the history of Guru Nanak and the *janam sakhi* tradition, or concerns over approaches to more modern aspects of Sikh history is a moot point. What is clear is that for Ahluwalia at least, history is important primarily for its impact on the present.

In the introduction to Kirpal Singh's study of the *janam sakhis*, Prithipal Singh Kapur explains that the *janam sakhi* literature is neither biography nor hagiography; they are compilations of anecdotes of the life of Guru Nanak. The different versions are understood as "parallel versions of the anecdotes concerning the life of Guru Nanak and were not written primarily in the interest of history in the modern sense of the word." While authenticity and historical credibility were important to the compilers, the primary intention in compiling them is to inspire faith in Guru Nanak and his teachings (2004, 13).

It is clear that Kirpal Singh (2004) regards the *janam sakhi* tradition as historical, and that he condemns the prejudice of Western scholars who have disregarded the possibility of historicity because of their metaphysical preconceptions. He argues there are archaeological finds that indicate the authenticity of the accounts of the Guru's travels that are found in the *janam sakhi* literature. Thus, there is an historical core at the heart of the *janam sakhi* tradition; that is to say, these are not arbitrary myths, legends or hagiographies, but carefully produced theological accounts of history.

Toby Johnson's proposal

In his PhD dissertation, Johnson (2015) argues that the *janam sakhis* should be primarily understood as a pedagogical tool. He explains:

> While the hymns of the Adi Granth (the primary scriptural text of Sikhism) are the formal lessons of the Guru's revelations, defining both a specific relationship with the divine reality and a moral program for Sikhs, the janam sakhis are the introduction to those lessons, serving as a prolegomenon that informs community's regard for the formal teachings ... The janam

sakhis emerged as historical literature in the late 16th Century, coalescing from an oral tradition about Guru Nanak. They became the primary expression of Guru Nanak's life and actions, operating initially as both records of his traditions and as a means of outreach for the growing community (2015, 11-12).

Johnson goes on to explain that the *janam sakhis* "do not present a necessarily coherent or sustained vision of Guru Nanak's life" and nor do the different traditions entirely agree with each other (2015, 14). This is, he proposes, because of the different authorial intentions and purpose in writing. Overall, the *janam sakhis* are understood as a history not just of the Guru, but of the whole Sikh community, written as "a story that both unites and motivates the Panth to act in accordance with their tradition and faith" (2015, 24). But the main focus is on providing a context for the teachings in the *Adi Granth*. As Johnson explains

> The story form of the janam sakhis, setting up a situation (or plot) which leads to Guru Nanak's recitation of new bani (sared utterances, collected in the hymns of the Adi Granth), helps to coordinate and sustain the learning effort of Sikhs. The stories are constructed lessons, tying Guru Nanak's actions to his message through the narrative. Janam sakhi narratives often provide the context for and rationale behind the Guru's hymns, or they can help Sikhs realize how their own actions can be informed by and derived from the Guru's inspiration. Guru Nanak becomes a reader's guru; he is their teacher (2015, 27).

This final point, that through the *janam sakhis* the Guru becomes the teacher of individual Sikhs is crucial for understanding their function; they are not objective history, but relational stories, written to help Sikhs know the Guru "as a more complete person than he is presented via his hymns in the *Adi Granth*" (2015, 28).

Johnson surveys the history of the different collections, as well as outlining some of the different scholarly approaches to these texts. He also explores different modes of presentation of the *janam sakhis,* including graphic novels aimed at children and teenagers, websites and both popular and more academic writings. A particular focus of his analysis is the frequency with which different stories are cited, and it is this part of his analysis that will be utilised as the discussion progresses. Johnson identifies twenty-four stories that appear in more than seventy-five per cent of the sources. He follows the accepted academic convention of using McLeod's classificatory scheme, producing the following table (2015, 366):

Sakhi	Count	Percent	Rank
124. Saidpur: Lalo and Bhago	30	86%	1
16. *Khara sauda:* the feeding of Sant Ren and the faqirs	30	86%	1
34. Hardwar: the watering of his fields	28	80%	3
22. Immersion in the river: his call	27	77%	4
5. Investiture with the sacred thread	23	66%	5
60. Sajjan the *thag*	22	63%	6
79. Mecca: the moving mosque	22	63%	6
122. *Panja Sahib*: the rock stopped	22	63%	6
6. The restored field	21	60%	9
8. The cobra's shadow	19	54%	10
21. Work in Daulat Khan's commissariat	19	54%	10

3. Instruction by the pandit	18	51%	12
25. Discourse with the qazi	17	49%	13
58. The cannibal's cauldron	17	49%	13
83. The sack of Saidpur	17	49%	13
114. Duni Chand's flags	17	49%	13
48. Jagannath Puri	16	46%	17
84. Discourse with Babur	15	43%	18
23. Nanak accused of embezzlement	14	40%	19
1. The birth of Guru Nanak	13	37%	20
4. Instruction by the mullah	13	37%	20
10. Betrothal and marriage	13	37%	20
11. The physician convinced	13	37%	20
72. Mount Sumeru	13	37%	20

This table will form the framework for the discussion in subsequent chapters. Each of these *janam sakhis* will be discussed in turn. The story will be cited, using the report given in one of the authors discussed above; a similar, or contrasting, text or story from the New Testament will be juxtaposed, and then the two accounts analysed. The focus of analysis is on the final form of the text(in the case of the New Testament) and on the story as received (in the case of the *janam sakhis*). This by-passing of discussions about authenticity or historicity of the accounts is a deliberate move, one adopted by numerous scholars. The focus is on how the text is read, not on how the text came to be.

Chapter 5

Discussion of the five most popular *Janam Sakhis*

This chapter will discuss what Johnson (2015) suggests are the five commonly cited *janam sakhis*, juxtaposing the accounts of the life of Guru Nanak with stories of Jesus' ministry as recorded in the four canonical Gospels of the New Testament. The decision to focus on five *janam sakhis* in this chapter is an arbitrary one made for the practical purpose of ensuring the chapter is a manageable length; chapter six discusses six *sakhis*, primarily because, according to Johnson's research, three *sakhis* are equally popular in tenth place, occurring in fifty-four per cent of the sources he examined.

According to Johnson, the two most popular *janam sakhis* are the Guru's encounter with Lalo and Bhago at Saidpur and the feeding of Sant Ren and the faqirs. Both occurred in eighty-six percent of the sources Johnson utilised in his research. I will recount each in turn.

THE FIVE MOST POPULAR JANAM SAKHIS

Saidpur: Lalo and Bhago[1]

As Guru Nanak travelled with his companion Mardana, the first place he stopped was Saidpur, now known as Eminabad. In that town he met a poor carpenter called Lalo. Nanak saw that Lalo was a hardworking and honest man, who made his living through his own physical effort. He was greatly impressed with Lalo's attitude, and resolved to stay with him while he was in Saidpur.

The news that a holy man had come to Saidpur and was staying with the lowly carpenter Lalo reached the ears of the town chief, Malik Bhago. Bhago was a corrupt and greedy man who exploited the poor and vulnerable of the town. Malik Bhago's pride was offended by Guru Nanak's decision to stay with Lalo and not with him.

One day, Bhago arranged a great feast, and invited all of the holy men of the town, including Guru Nanak, to attend. But the Guru declined the invitation. Bhago sent servants with choice dishes specifically for Nanak to eat, but he refused to accept these. Confused and upset, Bhago requested that Guru Nanak come and see him. The Guru agreed, and attended Bhago in his house, where Bhago enquired of Guru Nanak why he would not eat his food, and chose instead to eat the hard dry bread of Lalo the poor carpenter.

The Guru replied that the food which Malik Bhago considered to be tasty was in fact made out of the blood of the poor, that is, through exploitation and unfair means. By contrast, Lalo's food was made with money he had earned for himself. Although it was plain, it in fact tasted better, because it was procured through honest means.

1. The account of the incident in Saidpur which follows is based on that found in Johnson (2015, 57, who refers to his source as Shyam Dua, ed. *The Luminous Life of Guru Nanak Dev Ji* (Delhi: Tiny Tot publications, 2004), 28-30) and the account at https://www.allaboutsikhs.com/sikh-youth/guru-sakhis/malik-bhago-and-bhai-lalo/. Accessed 25th June 2021.

Saidpur: Lalo and Bhago

Bhago was furious at this comparison, and challenged the Guru to prove his point. The Guru sent for a loaf of bread from Lalo's house. Once it was brought, he held Lalo's bread in one hand and Bhago's bread in the other, and squeezed them both. While milk came out of Lalo's bread, blood dripped from Bhago's, thus proving the difference sources of their food. Malik Bhago was convicted of his guilt and asked the Guru for forgiveness. Guru Nanak's response was to tell him to distribute his wealth amongst the poor, and to live an honest and upright life from that day forward. Thus, Bhago was reborn through his encounter with the Guru's teaching and his grace.

The first story from Jesus' ministry that comes to my mind as resonating with this story is the encounter with Zacchaeus, which is recorded in Luke 19:1-10. Zacchaeus was a tax collector who lived in Jericho. A short man, who had made himself rich by exploiting his position and authority, he was unable to see Jesus, because of the crowd that had gathered to witness Jesus' arrival. Zacchaeus therefore climbed a sycamore tree and watched for Jesus from this vantage point. When the story is depicted for children, it is normal for Zacchaeus to be shown as hidden away, but there is no textual evidence to support this bit of added colour.

Whether Zacchaeus was hidden or in plain sight, he attracted Jesus' attention, because he stopped at the foot of the tree and told Zacchaeus to get down quickly and prepare a meal for him, because he wanted to eat at Zacchaeus' house that day. Zacchaeus duly complied, and provided a meal for Jesus. Those who saw Jesus' actions were upset and complained that Jesus was eating with a notorious sinner. Zacchaeus' response was to admit his guilt and offer to make reparation; giving to the poor and paying back anyone whom he has defrauded four times the amount he took. Jesus concluded: "Today salvation has come to this house, because he too is a son of Abraham. For the Son of Man came to seek out and to save the lost" (Luke 19:9-10, NRSV).

Both stories share the basic point, of a corrupt and exploitative figure being transformed through an encounter with a good and holy teacher. But there are striking differences between them. First, Jesus actively seeks out an opportunity to eat with the sinner Zacchaeus, whilst Guru Nanak refuses to eat Malik Bhago's food because it was produced from the blood of the poor. This suggests a different attitude to the possibility of ritual impurity, or perhaps a different understanding of the impact of the holiness of the teacher. Does Jesus eat with Zacchaeus because he is unconcerned about the polluting aspect of his food being derived from exploitation of the poor? Or is Jesus confident that his very presence will bring about the necessary change in Zacchaeus, and so redeem the corruption of the food? We can but speculate as to Jesus' motivations, although Luke's gospel contains a number of stories of Jesus sharing "table fellowship" with those who are identified as sinners and outcasts.

Another example that occurs earlier in Luke is Jesus' meal at the house of Simon the Pharisee (Luke 7:36-49). This is, of course, a meal at the house of a holy man. There is no suggestion in Luke's Gospel that Simon's piety is in question. What Jesus challenges is his attitude to the poor. Whilst Jesus is eating a "sinful woman" (7:37) comes and washes his feet with her tears, dries them with her hair and then anoints them with expensive perfume. This was regarded as scandalous and inappropriate behaviour, and Simon is outraged at what takes place. Jesus rebukes him, pointing out that Simon has not provided any water for Jesus to wash his feet (a normal courtesy for any guest), nor given him the expected kiss or anointing of the head with olive oil, greetings given to an honoured visitor. Jesus tells a short parable, in which one person is forgiven a small debt and the other a much larger debt. The point is that those who are forgiven much will love much. Simon, not conscious of being forgiven much, shows only a little love, while the "sinful woman," conscious of the depth of the forgiveness she has experienced, gives much more.

This story serves to emphasise a difference with the tale of the Guru's encounter with Lalo and Bhago; whilst Nanak prefers association with the righteous poor (something Jesus also does), Jesus is prepared to accept gifts and service from those who are known to be corrupt and sinful. This contrast is further emphasised in the second *sakhi*, the *Sacha Sauda*.

Sacha Sauda

The account of the *Sacha Sauda* (or "true bargain"), also known as *Khara Sauda* (the "good bargain"), is joint most-popular of all the *janam sakhis*, according to Johnson's research. There is some dispute about the details of the story (notably over the name of the Guru's companion and the identity of those whom he fed),[2] but the main point is clear.

This incident occurs much earlier in the Guru's life than the one recorded above. At this point, Guru Nanak is still living with his parents, working taking care of cattle. Guru Nanak does not find this employment fulfilling, and gives up on it. Instead of earning an income, Nanak spends his time in the company of holy men, enjoying religious discourse and debate. His father, worried that this is no way to make a living, attempts to persuade Guru Nanak to devote himself to the more mundane but necessary preoccupations of making a living, getting married and having a family. But the attempt backfires spectacularly.

His father gave Nanak twenty rupees, and told him to travel to the nearest town to buy goods which could then

---

2. Contrast the discussion in Johnson (2015, 51) with that of https://www.panthic.org/articles/3309. I have followed Johnson's version. (Accessed 25th June 2021).

THE FIVE MOST POPULAR *JANAM SAKHIS*

be sold at a profit. Guru Nanak sets off with a friend Bhai Bala (although other sources identify the companion as Bhai Mardana) towards the town of Chuharkana (Talwindi) in order to try their luck at business. But on the way there, they encounter a group of hungry sadhus (holy men; other sources suggest the group were starving, disease-afflicted children). Once he had encountered this needy group, Guru Nanak was moved with compassion, and promptly spent his father's money on providing for their needs. Returning empty handed, Guru Nanak was rebuked by his father for being so profligate and wasteful. But the Guru's response was that the best bargain he could strike is one in which those in need are cared for.

This is a foundational event in the establishment of Sikhi because it enshrines the principles of *dan* (charity) and *seva* (service) in a story that can easily be told to anyone of any age or intellectual ability. Thus, a core teaching of Sikhi, which is manifest in the *langar* as well as other acts of service, is promulgated in a simple tale of the generosity of Guru Nanak.

The most illuminating contrast within Christian teaching is possibly Jesus' "new command" to his disciples during the Johannine "Farewell Discourse." This long body of text, running from chapters thirteen to seventeen of John's Gospel, contains a wealth of teaching of Christian doctrine. The discourse begins with Jesus' enacted parable of washing his disciples' feet. He summarises the teaching of this parable in a command to the disciples to love one another. Jesus says, "Just as I have loved you, you also should love one another. By this everyone will know that you are my disciples, if you have love for one another" (John 13:34-35, NRSV).

One significant difference to note is that the Johannine command is primarily internally focused; loving service of one another within the Christian community is a witness to outsiders of the transformative power of following Christ.

Sacha Sauda

There are also externally focused commands to love sacrificially; the compassionate Samaritan who risks being mugged himself to provide for the needs of a mugged Jewish person, a potential mortal enemy, is a case in point (Luke 10:25-37).

A third potential (negative) contrast is the rich young ruler. Like the lawyer in the parable of the compassionate Samaritan, this man comes to Jesus, enquiring as to what is necessary to do in order to attain eternal life (Mark 10:17-27 and parallels). Jesus tells the man to keep the commandments, to not murder or commit adultery, to not steal or give false testimony or defraud, and to honour his parents. The exemplary young man states he has kept all these commands since his youth. Jesus' response is to tell him that he still lacks one thing: he must sell all he possesses, give the proceeds to the poor, and then come, follow Jesus.

This challenge is too much for the man, who "was shocked and went away grieving, for he had many possessions" (Mark 10:22, NRSV). The disciples, who like many of their contemporaries interpreted wealth as a sign of God's favour and blessing, are also shocked and distraught, asking Jesus who can be saved. Jesus tells them a joke, about the impossibility of a camel going through the eye of a needle, to reinforce his teaching that wealth is not a sign of God's blessing. Salvation and blessing are gifts from God, given to those he chooses.

For the purposes of the contrast with the *janam sakhi* of the better bargain, it is notable that in both cases, attachment to wealth and a desire to be financially comfortable are hindrances, not helps, to spiritual process and relationship with the divine. In a sense, Guru Nanak passes the test which the rich young ruler fails, giving away all the money he has in service of God. Such generosity is also found in the widow who gives all her wealth to the temple (Mark 12:41-44; Luke 21:1-4), although her focus is on a different kind of worship. Thus both Guru Nanak, and Jesus(who commends the widow's actions) teach that money does not help you come closer to the divine.

Hardwar: the watering of the Guru's fields[3]

According to Johnson's research, the third most popular *sakhi*, occurring in eighty per cent of the sources he surveyed is the account of the Guru at Hardwar. Kirpal Singh explains that Guru Nanak travelled with his companion Mardana to Hardwar, which was crowded with people gathering for the Vaisakhi fair. Guru Nanak joined the pilgrims who were standing in the waters of the river, but whilst they were offering water to the east, towards the sun, he began throwing water westwards. This action confused those gathered, who speculated as to why he was doing this, wondering if he was a Muslim. They resolved to ask him why he, who by all appearances was a man of God, was not following the expected convention of throwing water eastwards. When questioned as to why he was throwing water westwards, Guru Nanak replied with a question, as to why they were throwing water eastwards towards the sun.

The pilgrims replied that they were offering water to their ancestors. Guru Nanak enquired where these ancestors lived, and was told they lived "in the older world, about 490 million *kos* away" (that is, about 98 million kilometres or 61 million miles away). The Guru then asked if the water that was being thrown reached the ancestors, and his interlocutors replied in the affirmative. Guru Nanak then explained that he had lands near Lahore (around 400 km or 250 miles away), and that he was sending water to those fields. His audience laughed at him, mockingly questioning him as to how

---

3. The account that follows is based on that found in Kirpal Singh (2004, 91).

Hardwar: the watering of the Guru's fields

the water would reach Lahore, which they assured him was too distant to be reached. The Guru's response was that the water would reach his fields in Lahore in the same way that the pilgrim's water reached their ancestors.

Johnson (2015, 99) adds that the Guru's visit to Hardwar involved not simply this debate over throwing water as an offering, but also, according to the Miharban *janam sakhi*, an incident later in the evening. A brahmin prepared food for Guru Nanak, but the Guru's travelling companion, Mardana, who was a Muslim, violated the purity of the brahmin's cooking square, thus polluting his food. Not realising that Mardana was Guru Nanak's travelling companion, the brahmin nevertheless offered the food to Guru Nanak. The Guru refused to accept it, saying it was polluted. When the brahmin protested that it was not, Guru Nanak responded, saying four *chandalas* (low caste) had entered the square, namely perversity of mind, lack of compassion, desire and anger.

Taken together, these two incidents point towards a focus on both purity and also an avoidance of empty ritual. Guru Nanak is concerned not with outward appearances of piety, or completion of actions purely for the sake of public display of religiosity. Rather his focus is on the attitude of the heart and on cultivating an inner piety and purity of intention. Johnson points out this understanding is summarised in a verse from the Adi Granth:

> Make the practice of virtue your cooking square, make meditation on God's name the ceremonial washing of your body. Those alone shall be considered good and pure who do not walk in the path of impure conduct (AG 91, as cited in Johnson 2015, 99).

Ritual piety is therefore rejected as inadequate for attaining a truly holy and righteous way of living.

THE FIVE MOST POPULAR *JANAM SAKHIS*

There are at least three points of connection with the stories of Jesus as told in the four canonical Gospels. The first resonance is with Jesus' condemnation of the religious hypocrisy of certain leaders in Matthew 23. Jesus charges the scribes and the Pharisees with adding unnecessary extra burdens to religious obligations, requirements they expect others to follow but do not observe themselves. He rebukes them for focusing on ostentatious displays of piety that will draw attention to the outward form of their religious devotion, and for avoiding the weighty obligations of the Torah towards justice and mercy while providing loop holes that allow others to fulfil the letter but not the spirit of the Torah. Jesus' condemnations are forthright:

> Woe to you, scribes and Pharisees, hypocrites! For you are like whitewashed tombs, which on the outside look beautiful, but inside they are full of the bones of the dead and of all kinds of filth. So, you also on the outside look righteous to others, but inside you are full of hypocrisy and lawlessness. (Matthew 23:27-28, NRSV)

Jesus concludes that whilst these leaders observe the outward forms of piety in honouring the tombs of the prophets and the graves of the righteous, they have not taken to heart the message that those holy men brought. Their piety is thus empty and meaningless, much as the water offerings to the sun or the concern for ritual purity of food are irrelevant.

Second, Jesus is also questioned about rules regarding the consumption of food. Judaism has clear stipulations about what can and cannot be eaten, not only in an absolute sense (pork is prohibited entirely, for example), but also in a relative sense, notably that milk products cannot be mixed with meat. That is to say provided, for example, a lamb was slaughtered according to the appropriate religious requirements, it could be eaten, but not accompanied by any dairy products.

Hardwar: the watering of the Guru's fields

In Mark 7, Jesus is questioned by some scribes and Pharisees, who enquire as to why Jesus' disciples had not washed their hands before eating. Jesus responds first with a quote from the Prophet Isaiah, who condemned those who honoured God with their speech whilst their hearts were distant from him. Jesus then condemned those who sought to find exceptions or loopholes in the observation of the Torah, before explaining to the crowd that "There is nothing outside a person that by going in can defile, but the things that come out are what defile" (Mark 7:15, NRSV). His disciples did not fully understand what this meant, and questioned Jesus in private. He explained that food, which is taken into the body, passed out through the body and into a sewer does not defile. Rather what makes a person impure are the evil intentions that come from the heart, "fornication, theft, murder, adultery, avarice, wickedness, deceit, licentiousness, envy, slander, pride, folly" (Mark 7:21-22, NRSV).

The rejection of categories of ritually impure food is a major preoccupation of the New Testament, taking up several chapters in the Acts of the Apostles, starting with Peter's vision in Acts 10 and continuing through discussions held by the leaders of the Jerusalem Church. The Apostle Paul is forthright in his rejection of the Jewish food laws, both in Galatians 2:11-21, as well as Romans 14:1-4 and 1 Corinthians 8:1-13). This is a distinctive feature of Christian faith; most other major religious systems include prohibition of certain food types. As Mandair explains, whilst there are no hard-and-fast rules within the Guru Granth Sahib concerning diet, no meat or intoxicants will be served in a gurdwara. Moreover, some Khalsa orders require strict vegetarianism. The Sikh Code of Conduct does not itself prohibit the consumption of meat, but there is a prohibition against meat that has been slaughtered according to the requirements of Islamic law. Provided an animal has been slaughtered with a single stroke, the meat can be eaten. Sikhs generally also avoid eating beef. Whilst drug and tobacco use are prohibited and alcohol is to be avoided because of its intoxicant potential, the reality is that some Sikhs do drink or smoke (2013, 171-72). Hindus are likewise mainly vegetarian, and even those who do eat meat would never eat beef. At the very least, Muslims will not eat pork or drink alcohol; the full requirements of a halal diet are much stricter.

The third resonance links with the first. When commending the practise of spiritual disciplines, specifically fasting, prayer and almsgiving, Jesus is clear that these actions are to be performed privately (Matthew 6:1-18). While the Gentiles and the hypocrites draw attention to their piety, Jesus commands his disciples to do so in secret, so that their Father in Heaven, who sees what is done in secret, may reward them. The point is thus not a prohibition on a devout life, but rather an injunction that a devout life is a personal not a public matter.

Guru Nanak's immersion in the river: his call[4]

It is striking that within Johnson's ranking system, the Guru's call is fourth not first. It might be expected that this is the most popular of all the stories, as it is the account of the birth of the Sikh faith.

Guru Nanak experienced his call while at Sultanpur. He was in the habit of going to the river Bein early in the morning to bathe. One morning he did not return from washing, and it was feared he had drowned. The Guru appeared on the bank of the river on the third day. The Puratan *janam sakhi*

---

4. The full account below is that cited by Johnson (2015, 16-18), reproducing the work Nikky-Guninder Kaur Singh, "The Myth of the Founder: The Janamsakhis and Sikh Tradition," *History of Religions* 31.4(1992), 331-34

Guru Nanak's immersion in the river: his call

records that he had spent the intervening period in the presence of the Supreme Being. At the conclusion of his experience of revelation, Guru Nanak was offered a cup filled with *amrit* (nectar), which he drank in response to this command:

> this is the cup of Name-adoration. Drink it... I am with you and I do bless and exalt you. Whoever remembers you will have my favour. Go, rejoice, in My Name and teach others to do so... I have bestowed upon you the gift of My Name. Let this be your calling.

Kaur Singh explains that the separation is clear; Guru Nanak leaves behind everything when he goes to bathe; his clothes, his place in society, his family. He is then in a liminal state, no longer the employee of his Muslim master, but not yet the Guru who will be followed by millions. During this transitional three-day period, Nanak comes into the divine presence, and receives a cup of Amrit, the drink of immortality (*a* = not, *mrit* = death). Kaur Singh explains that Nanak does not see the Divine, but merely hears the Divine voice whilst in the river. Nanak is also tested, through an instruction to demonstrate his approach to sharing the revelation he has received. He recites a poem of praise which proves he is worthy; once this is accepted Nanak then recites his *Jap,* which contains the core of his creed. The final element of the liminal process is for Nanak to receive the dress and initiation of a Guru. He is then reincorporated into society, or as Kaur Singh puts it, creating an "antistructure" of society which shatters the divisions and hierarchies of society. This is most clearly seen in the development of *seva* (service), *langar* (the community meal) and *sangat* (the Sikh congregation). The Sikhs had no ordination or priests, but all were to develop their own relationship with the divine (2011, 8-11).

Guru Nanak celebrated his experience of divine favour through a song of praise:

THE FIVE MOST POPULAR *JANAM SAKHIS*

Were I to live for millions of years
and could make air my food and drink,
Were I to seal myself in a cave and ceaselessly to meditate
without seeing the sun or the moon and without a wink of sleep,
I would still not be able to measure Your greatness,
nor signify the glory of Your Name!

The Formless One is the eternal, irreplaceable truth,
Attempt not to describe That by hearsay knowledge.
If it pleases It, It in Its grace will reveal Itself.
Were I to be shredded and ground like grain in a mill,
Were I to be burnt in a fire and reduced to ashes,

I would not be able to measure Your greatness,
nor signify the glory of Your Name!

Were I to fly like a bird to a hundred heavens,
Were I to vanish from human gaze at will
and could live without food and drink,
I would still not be able to measure Your greatness,
nor signify the glory of Your Name!

Had there been ton upon ton of paper, says Nanak,
and had I absorbed the wisdom of volumes beyond count,
If I had a supply of ink inexhaustible and I could write with the speed of the wind,
I would still not be able to measure Your greatness,

Guru Nanak's immersion in the river: his call

> nor signify the glory of Your Name! (Johnson 2015, 16-18).

Once he had recited this praise to the divine, the Supreme Being spoke to him, saying "Nanak, you discern My will." In response, the Guru recited the *Japji*, which encapsulated the core of his teaching, and thus became the opening text of the Adi Granth.

> The Supreme Being spoke again: "Who is just in your eyes, Nanak, shall be so in Mine. Whoever receives your grace shall abide in Mine. My name is the Supreme God; your name is the divine Guru."

Guru Nanak then bowed in gratitude and a second song was heard:

> The skies are the platter; sun and moon, lamps; stars, the pearls.
> The breeze is the incense; entire verdure, a bouquet of flowers.
> What an arati!
> The Wonder of wonders, Sunderer of the circuit of life and death.
> Thine splendid arati!
> Primal music is playing motionlessly.
> You have a thousand eyes, but without eyes You are,
> You have a thousand forms, but without form You are,
> You have a thousand feet, but without feet You are.
> You have a thousand noses, but without a nose You are.

THE FIVE MOST POPULAR *JANAM SAKHIS*

> Thoroughly enchanted am I.
> There is a light in all and that light is That One.
> From Its light, all are illumined.
> Through the Guru the light becomes visible.
> What pleases You, becomes Your arati!
> Like the bumble-bee, day and night I long for
> your lotus-feet.
> Pleads Nanak, grant the thirsty bird, the nectar
> of Your Name.

Guru Nanak did not speak further for the whole day after his reappearance. When he spoke the following day, the first words he uttered were: "There is no Hindu; there is no Musalman." The Guru's first words are the foundations of the Sikh understanding of equality and rejection of the religious systems which preceded the Guru.

For a Christian, there is an immediate resonance in the mention of the "third day," which echoes the fact that Jesus rose from the dead on the third day after his crucifixion. This is, however, not an especially substantial parallel. There is a greater connection with Jesus' baptism. Each of the four Gospels add a different point to this momentous public event. In Mark, the account is brief:

> In those days Jesus came from Nazareth of Galilee and was baptized by John in the Jordan. And just as he was coming up out of the water, he saw the heavens torn apart and the Spirit descending like a dove on him. And a voice came from heaven, "You are my Son, the Beloved; with you I am well pleased" (Mark 1:9-11, NRSV).

The main points are the involvement of the Trinity: the Spirit descends on the Son whilst the Father speaks approval and blessing on the Son. Jesus then goes into the desert,

Guru Nanak's immersion in the river: his call

where he is tempted before returning, calling people to repentance and faith, for "the time is fulfilled and the kingdom of God has come near" (Mark 1:15, NRSV).

In Matthew's Gospel, there is an added preamble, in which John the Baptist initially refuses to baptise Jesus, saying that he, John, needs to be baptised by Jesus, not the other way around. But Jesus persuades John this is the correct approach, as by being baptised, Jesus will "fulfil all righteousness" (Matthew 3:15, NRSV). This phrase is indicative of Matthew's concern to ensure that Jesus' every action is seen as fulfilling the plans and purposes of God as revealed in the Hebrew Scriptures. It is therefore a further way of signalling the nature and extent of Jesus' authority, which is confirmed by the Father's words, which are the same as those in Mark cited above.

In Luke the twist is that the Holy Spirit descends on Jesus "in bodily form like a dove" (Luke 3:22, NRSV), emphasising further the physically transformative nature of the Trinitarian relationship that is manifested at this point in Jesus' ministry. After his account of the temptations in the desert, Luke then records Jesus returning to Nazareth, where he attends synagogue on the Sabbath, as was his custom. Jesus is asked to read from the Prophet Isaiah, and he does so, speaking these words:

> The Spirit of the Lord is upon me,
>   because he has anointed me
>   to bring good news to the poor.
> He has sent me to proclaim release to the captives
>   and recovery of sight to the blind,
>   to let the oppressed go free,
> to proclaim the year of the Lord's favour. (Luke 4:18-19, NRSV).

Generations of Christian theologians have examined this short text exhaustively and limitations of space preclude a detailed discussion here. The main point to note is that Jesus speaks of transformative peace and justice but that he stops before Isaiah's reference to the vengeance of God. The message is therefore primarily one of grace and hope for all people, regardless of ethnicity.

In John there is no direct reference to a baptism ceremony, but when questioned as to his own identity, John the Baptist responds by saying that he saw the Spirit of God descending like a dove and remaining on Jesus, which enables John the Baptist to testify that Jesus is the one who baptises with the Holy Spirit and is also the Son of God.

Jesus' baptism is therefore both similar to, but also markedly different from, Guru Nanak's immersion and subsequent three-day absence. Both are clearly the point of departure for an itinerant teaching ministry, which calls disciples but also engenders great controversy. Both experience the divine at this particular moment of call, but the nature of that experience differs, arguably because the Christian understanding of Jesus as God manifest in human form is very different from the Sikh understanding of Guru Nanak as the messenger who speaks the words of God.

Investiture with the sacred thread[5]

According to Johnson's analysis, the fifth most popular *janam sakhi* is the account of Guru Nanak's response to the sacred thread tying ceremony. The ceremony, known as *janeu*, is performed on upper-caste(Brahmin) Hindus for their male children, putting on a thread woven of seven cotton

---

5. Johnson (2015, 50), who cites his source as Roopinder Singh, Guru Nanak: His Life & Teachings (New Delhi: Rupa & Co, 2007), 13-14.

Investiture with the sacred thread

strings as a sign of being "twice-born," that is, both physically born and also entering into a discipleship relationship with one's Guru. It is a significant moment in the life of a child, a form of coming-of-age ceremony, celebrated in the company of the extended family and well-wishers.

Nanak's father arranged for this ceremony to take place for him, but when Pandit Hardyal, the family priest, attempted to place the thread on Nanak's left shoulder, as is usually done, Nanak caught the thread in his hands, and asked what would be the advantage of putting it on. The Pandit explained that it was necessary as a sign he was a high caste Hindu. Nanak then refused to wear it, saying it should be actions, not a badge of rank or status that should be used to distinguish between people. The assembled company were shocked and surprised at Nanak's response. To clarify what he meant, Nanak then recited the following hymn, to explain what *janeu* ought to be:

> Let compassion be your cotton!
> Spin it into the yarn of contentment;
> Give it knots of continence,
> And the twist of truth,
> Thus will you make a *janeu* for the soul.
> If such a one you have,
> Put it on me.
> The thread so made will neither snap, nor become soiled.
> It will neither be burned nor lost.
> Blessed is the man, O Nanak,
> Who wears such a thread around his neck!

Other sources give a fuller account of this incident, in which Nanak debates with the Pandit, who is shocked at the behaviour of one whom he regards as an impudent young boy. Nanak's response to the challenge to explain why he rejects *janeu* is unequivocal:

> Though men commit countless thefts, countless adulteries, utter countless falsehoods and countless words of abuse;
> Though they commit countless robberies and villanies night and day against their fellow creatures;
> Yet the cotton thread is spun, and the Brahman cometh to twist it.
> For the ceremony they kill a goat and cook and eat it, and everybody then saith "Put on the janeu."
> When it becometh old, it is thrown away, and another is put on, Nanak, the string breaketh not if it be strong.[6]

The core teaching, of rejection of religious ritual as empty and meaningless and advocacy of purity of heart and action is common to other *janam sakhis* discussed above. What is striking in this story is the Guru's decision to reject family expectations at such a young age.

Aside from the birth narratives, there is only one story of Jesus' childhood in the four canonical gospels,[7] found in Luke 2:41-51. It describes how Jesus' family were in the habit of travelling to Jerusalem each year to celebrate the Passover festival. When Jesus was twelve years old, the family went to Jerusalem as usual. When they set out to return home, Jesus remained in Jerusalem, and his parents travelled for a whole day before they realised this had happened. This may seem unlikely to modern readers, but it should be noted that it is probable that the men and women travelled separately, and that Jesus was on the cusp of manhood. Thus, Mary presumably thought Jesus was with the men, and Joseph that he was

---

6. Source: https://www.sikhiwiki.org/index.php/Guru_Nanak_and_the_Sacred_Thread Accessed 25th June 2021.
7. The apocryphal Gospels and other non-canonical scriptures contain numerous other stories, but as they are not recognised by the Christian community as authentic stories of Jesus' life, they will not be considered here.

with the women, and it was only when they tried to gather as a family in the evening that the oversight was realised.

Mary and Joseph hurried back to Jerusalem and spent three days searching for him, eventually finding him in the Temple. Mary rebuked Jesus, asking him why he had treated them so badly, for they had been searching anxiously for him. Jesus responded, "Why were you searching for me? Did you not know that I must be in my Father's house?" [or "about my Father's interests?"] (Luke 2:49). He then returns obediently with his family to Nazareth and grows up in relative obscurity, until his public ministry begins eighteen years later.

According to Christian doctrine, Jesus is without sin; thus, this incident cannot be understood within a Christian theological framework as the actions of a child rebelling against the expectations of his parents. Rather, it is interpreted as a sign, at a young age, that Jesus was solely obedient to God his Father. The point is reinforced in other incidents, during Jesus public ministry, when his family come to speak with him, and he refuses to go out to see them, claiming that his family are those who follow the Father's will or refuses to head their advice and guidance, following his own agenda even when it differs from that of his family (Matthew 12:46-50; John 7:1-10).

Both Jesus and Guru Nanak followed the agenda they believed had been set for them by God. Whilst both lived in cultures where obedience to one's father was of social (and religious) importance, both were prepared to rebel against that expected norm out of devotion to a higher calling and power.

Reflections so far

The discussion of what Johnson (2015) classifies as the five most popular *janam sakhis* has yielded some useful points of connection between Sikh understandings of Guru Nanak and Christian understandings of Jesus Christ. Both are regarded as holy men, sent by God to accomplish a particular mission and walk a particular path. Both condemn empty religiosity and meaningless observation of ritual and both rebel against the expectations of their parents. Both are socially disruptive and challenge the comfortable norms and expectations of their own day.

It must also be acknowledged that the detail of those paths differs considerably, as has become clear even in this brief discussion. There are different understandings of expected purity, in particular around what can and cannot be eaten, as well as different stories of how they received their call and began their public ministry. They lived in very different times and contexts, and this must be borne in mind as the work of comparison continues.

Chapter 6

Sakhis in the ranking sixth to tenth most popular

In Johnson's analysis there are six *sakhis* in the ranking sixth to tenth most popular, with three occupying the position of joint sixth most popular, one ranked ninth, and two allocated joint tenth position. As in the previous chapter, each will be introduced and the meaning discussed, before possible resonances with Christian texts are discussed.

Sajjan the thag

In Kirpal Singh's account of Nanak's life (2004, 81-83), he explains that the Guru was asked to travel from Sayyadpur to Pakpatan, which took him through a town called Tulamba (now called Makhdoompur) on the bank on the river Ravi.

SIXTH TO TENTH MOST POPULAR *SAKHIS*

There was no place for travellers to stay other than a hostel constructed outside the town by a man named Sajjan. Kirpal Singh explains that Sajjan would welcome in travellers in order to kill them and steal their possessions. Guru Nanak halted there, appearing to accept Sajjan's hospitality. Invited by Sajjan to go to sleep, Nanak responded with this hymn:

> Tinned copper so bright and lustrous
> When rubbed, appears a surface inky black.
> Its impurity by washing shall not go, despite washing a hundred times.
> Those are true friends who are one's companions of the way.
> And when their reckoning is called for, instantly render it.
> Chambers, domes and bowers, painted all over,
> When crumbled are little good, found deserted within.
> Storks white-robed that at holy spots abide,
> Gripping creatures swallow them – such immaculate cannot be called.
> Like the cotton-wool tree is my body, that deludes parrots.
> Useless its fruit –
> Such are my qualities.
> I the blind man, carrying a heavy load, along mountain-path have to traverse.
> Nothing with my eyes can I behold –
> How may I ascend this path to cross?
> What good other devotion, merits and clever devices?
> Saith Nanak: Contemplate thou the Name, whereby from bonds mayst thou be freed (AG 729, cited in Singh 2004, 82).

Sajjan the thag

Singh goes on to explain that this hymn had a powerful effect on Sajjan, who experienced a profound revelation of his own evil actions and thoughts. Recognizing that Guru Nanak was a holy man, Sajjan repented before him and resolved from that day forward to live a righteous and holy life. This is one of a number of stories which illustrate the profound impact meeting Guru Nanak had on people of evil inclination. As with the example of Bhago discussed in the previous chapter, recognition of his own character and the impact of his actions caused Sajjan to change his behaviour.

The resonances with the life of Jesus are therefore similar to those already discussed, with the repentance of Zacchaeus providing one close parallel story. It is also worth noting the impact that meeting Jesus had on Saul, a persecutor of the early church, who through his Damascus Road experience went on to become Paul, preacher of the Christian faith *par excellence*. The full detail of Paul's conversion story does not need to be explored here; suffice to say he is introduced in Acts 7:58 as the one who looked after the coats of those who stoned Stephen, the first Christian martyr, to death. Acts 8 records Saul as "ravaging the church by entering house after house" and dragging the occupants, both men and women, off to prison (Acts 8:3). In Acts 9, Saul requests permission to go to Damascus to arrest Christians there (presumably because he has achieved what he wanted to in Jerusalem). On the way to Damascus, Paul has a vision of Jesus, and makes a complete turn in orientation, from persecutor to preacher of faith in Jesus as Messiah, and as a result becoming pursued himself by those who disagree with his new assessment of Jesus, as much of the book of Acts records.

It is unclear whether Sajjan (or Bhago for that matter) became active within the early Sikh community, and perhaps this personal shift is not the concern of the *janam sakhis*. But it is instructive to consider not just the moment when a person is convicted of the evil nature of their actions, but also what subsequent impact this has on their way of living.

SIXTH TO TENTH MOST POPULAR *SAKHIS*

Mecca: The Moving Mosque

One of the *janam sakhi* accounts of Guru Nanak's travels concerns his visit to Mecca. According to the tale, Nanak lay down to rest in front of the Ka'aba. The Ka'aba is the holiest site in Islam; a black cube of a building in Mecca, which prior to the time of the Prophet Muhammad, was filled with the idols that the local Quraysh tribe worshipped. When Muhammad took authority over the city, the Ka'aba was cleansed of the idols, and became the focal point of Muslim prayers. Wherever they pray in the world today, Muslims do so facing Mecca, and more specifically, towards the Ka'aba. It is revered as having been first built by Abraham and his son Ishmael, and is circumambulated seven times during the *hajj*.

It is thus the centre of devotional focus within Islam. Guru Nanak was rebuked by a religious leader because his feet were facing towards the Ka'aba, and this was understood as a sign of disrespect to the house of God. Guru Nanak did not become angry, but simply asked his interlocutor to move his feet to face in a direction which was not the dwelling place of God. The Muslims began to move Nanak's feet, but as they did so, the Ka'aba also moved, so whichever direction that Nanak's feet faced, the Ka'aba was found there. The assembled Muslims asked Nanak whether he was a Hindu or a Muslim. In reply, he uttered the following hymn:

> Lord! Thy fear is my hemp-drug, my mind the leather pouch.
> Mad is this intoxication, an anchorite am I become.
> With my bowl for Thy sight I beg, that I hunger for.
> This ever at Thy door I beg.
> For Thy sigh I yearn;

> At Thy door a beggar – pray dole out this charity to me.
> Saffron, flowers, musk and gold by all persons of all castes may be offered.
> The merit of sandalwood and God's devotees is,
> To all they impart fragrance.
> None considers ghee and silk polluted:
> Such is God's devotee, whatever his caste.
> These in devotion to Thy Name bow.
> Nanak at the door of such begs alms (AG 71, cited in Singh 2004, 189-90).

This response did not answer the Muslims' question, and so they asked Guru Nanak to show them the book he had under his arm, in the hope that it might be a Quran, which would have answered their enquiry. They also asked whether both Hindus and Muslims were good. Guru Nanak's response was that all would suffer if they did not perform noble deeds of righteousness, and he taught that all who do good are good people (Singh 2004, 190). Kaur Singh suggests that it is unnecessary to consider this incident to be historical. Rather, the point is metaphysical, "that the Divine exists in every direction and that internal religiosity cannot be expressed externally are effectively communicated" (2011, 6).

When Jesus debated religion with a Samaritan woman at a well outside her village, she turned the conversation towards the appropriate location for worship of God to take place, perhaps as a way of shifting the focus away from her own life. As a Samaritan, she believed that worship should take place on Mount Gerizim, whilst presuming that as a Jew, Jesus would be in favour of worship at Jerusalem. But Jesus rejected the premise that worship must be confined to a particular holy location. Rather, he argued, the time is coming, or has already come, when the location of worship will become irrelevant as those who truly worship the Father do so "in spirit and truth" (John 4:21-23).

SIXTH TO TENTH MOST POPULAR *SAKHIS*

There is a resonance in Jesus' teaching, that location of worship is less important than focus of worship, with Guru Nanak's point that the divine permeates everything, and as such there is no place where his feet would not point towards the divine presence. It should be noted that Jesus does express concern for the purity of the Temple, in that he is recorded as driving out those who were utilising the Court of the Gentiles, the outermost courtyard of the Jerusalem Temple, as a place to exchange money and sell animals for sacrifice. Commentators have debated the significance of Jesus' actions, including how to relate the incident in John 2:13-25 with that recorded in Mark 11:15-17; Matthew 21:12-17; and Luke 19:45-46. Each gospel records Jesus as returning to the Temple after this incident, so it is hard to see it as a complete rejection of the Temple as a place of worship. More likely, Jesus was concerned that the Court of the Gentiles, the only space those who are not of Jewish origin were able to pray, was not being used for the purpose of prayer. The problem was therefore not so much that money changing and sale of sacrificial animals was taking place, as with the location of those transactions. That is to say, whilst Jesus rejected the specificity of place of worship in his conversation with the Samaritan woman, he nevertheless wanted places dedicated to worship to be suitably accessible to everyone, regardless of ethnicity and gender.

A final point to note in relation to accessibility of the divine is that the Temple curtain was torn in two at the moment Jesus died (Matthew 27:51; Mark 15:38). The curtain separated the Holy of Holies, the place where God's presence was believed to be, from the rest of the Temple. The Holy of Holies was entered only once a year, when the High Priest performed the rituals associated with the Day of Atonement (Leviticus 16). The symbolism of the curtain being torn is that it indicates the Christian belief that once Jesus died on the cross, God can be accessed anywhere, through the mediation of the Son of God, Jesus Christ, not through the offices of any temple priest, a point explored at length in the Epistle to the Hebrews. This echoes Guru Nanak's point, that there is no direction for his feet to point where Waheguru is not already present.

Panja Sahib: The Rock Stopped

According to this *sakhi*, the Guru travelled with his companion Mardana to Hasan Abdal, a village in the Attock District, between Pawlpindi and Peshawar.[1] A Muslim holy man, Hazrat Shah Wali Qandhari lived at the top of a nearby hill, where there was also a spring of fresh water. There was no water available at the foot of the hill, and so Mardana climbed the hill in order to draw some water. Unfortunately, Wali Qandhari had heard of Guru Nanak, and was jealous of his reputation as a holy man, and so refused Mardana permission to collect any water. Mardana asked a second time, but was again rebuffed. This time Wali Qandhari suggested that Mardana returned to the bottom of the hill and ask his Guru to provide him with a drink, for surely so great a holy man could perform such a simple task.

Mardana returned to the foot of the hill and requested water from Guru Nanak, stating that he would rather die of thirst than climb the hill again and ask for water from Wali Qandhari. Guru Nanak did as Mardana requested, moving a rock aside and causing a spring of pure water to flow at the foot of the hill, while at the same time the spring at the summit dried up. The loss of his water supply enraged Wali Qandhari further, and he rolled a huge boulder down the hill towards Guru Nanak. But the Guru simply raised his hand, stopping the massive rock and leaving the mark of his hand on the rock. For this reason, the place is now known as *Panja*

---

1. This account is based on McLeod (1968, 78) and https://barusahib.org/general/17445/, accessed 29th June 2021.

SIXTH TO TENTH MOST POPULAR *SAKHIS*

Sahib, or Holy Palm, and is the site of a gurdwara built by Hari Singh Nalwa, a famous Sikh general. Mardana quenched his thirst and Wali Qandhari was so impressed by what he saw, that he too became a devotee of Guru Nanak.

There are two incidents in Jesus' life where he makes a significant miraculous provision of food, and one where he turns water into wine. This incident took place at a wedding in Cana in Galilee. Jesus and his disciples, as well as Jesus' mother Mary are all guests at the wedding. Mary realised the hosts had run out of wine and asks her son to solve the problem. He is initially reluctant, but subsequently orders the servants to fill six large stone jars with water, draw out the water and take it to their master. When they do so, the water has turned into wine, of much better quality than that which had been served initially (John 2:1-12). This miracle is the first of John's seven signs that point towards Jesus' status as the Son of God, and is interpreted as Jesus bringing the new wine of God's kingdom.

One of Jesus' two recorded feeding miracles involved five thousand Jewish men, as well as an uncounted number of women and children. This miracle is recorded in all four Gospels, one of very few to be given such prominence (Matthew 14:13-21; Mark 6:30-44; Luke 9:10-17; John 6:1-15). The miracle involves a boy's own lunch, of five small loaves of bread and two fish, being multiplied to provide food for the assembled throng, together with twelve baskets of leftovers. Jesus performs the miracle in a desert place at the festival of Passover, staking a theological claim to his identity as the new Moses, as well as demonstrating his miraculous power. The other miracle, where seven loaves of bread provide enough food for four thousand men in the Gentile dominated region of the Decapolis (Matthew 15:29-39) is of less theological importance, but still points to Jesus' power and identity as Son of God.

There are no miracles in the four Canonical Gospels where Jesus provides water, but miraculous provision of wa-

Panja Sahib: The Rock Stopped

ter is recorded in the Pentateuch as the people of Israel wander in the desert. There are two accounts, in Exodus 17 and Numbers 20. The first incident takes place not long after the people have fled Egypt, crossing the Red Sea and beginning to journey through the desert. They camp at a place called Rephidim, but there is no water there. This enrages the people of Israel, who quarrel with Moses, demanding water from him. He protests back, asking them why they are testing the Lord. As the people continue grumbling, Moses appeals to God for help. He is commanded to strike a rock with his staff. When he does so, water came out of it for the people of Israel to drink. The location of this incident is given at "by the rock at Horeb," that is, the mountain of God (Exodus 17:6). Moses calls the place *Massah*, which means "testing" and *Meribah*, which means "quarrelling." The incident is recounted in Psalm 95, as a sign that lack of faith in the Lord was the reason the generation which fled Egypt were unable to enter the Promised Land.

The second story, in Numbers 20, is perhaps a parallel account of the same incident, or may be another record of a similar event. The basic features are the same: the people complain there is no water, this time with greater reminiscing about the good food they enjoyed in Egypt but can access no longer. This time it is both Moses and Aaron who go before the Lord, who instructs them

> Take the staff, and assemble the congregation, you and your brother Aaron, and command the rock before their eyes to yield its water. Thus you shall bring water out of the rock for them; thus you shall provide drink for the congregation and their livestock (Numbers 20:8, NRSV).

Moses does as he has been instructed, striking the rock twice with his staff, which brings forth water, which everyone drinks from and is satisfied. There follows a specific rebuke to Moses and Aaron for their lack of faith; their punishment is that they also do not enter the Promised Land. The account closes with a reminder that these are the waters of *Meribah*, quarrelling, where Israel testing the Lord.

The two water-from-a-rock miracles in the Old Testament have a different focus from the miraculous provision made by Guru Nanak. The main point is that the people of Israel showed a lack of faith by demanding water; they should have trusted that the Lord would provide. But there is no similar suggestion in Guru Nanak's response to Mardana's thirst. Indeed, he is quite happy providing for his disciple. The underlying principle, of divine provision of material needs through particular chosen leaders and holy men is arguably the same in all the miracles discussed above. The difference is primarily in the attitude of those asking. Exodus and Numbers focus on the grumbling of a reluctant people, the Gospels mainly on surprise and unexpected provision, while the *janam sakhi* celebrates on the faith of the one who asked.

The Restored Field

The account of the restored field is an incident in Guru Nanak's childhood. He was put in charge of a herd of buffaloes, but did not pay attention to what they were doing. While Nanak was lost in meditation, the buffaloes destroyed a neighbour's crops. The neighbour was devastated by what happened, for the crops were his livelihood; without them he faced poverty and despair. Moved with compassion at the man's need, the young Nanak promised that God would provide a blessing on his field. Unsurprisingly this reassurance was unpersuasive, and the owner of the field appealed to the village chief, Rai Bular, for compensation.

The Restored Field

Rai Bular sent men to examine the damage and estimate what a reparation would cost. But when they arrived at the field, they found it undamaged, and returned to Rai Bular to report this. The farmer protested that he had seen his field damaged, but ultimately was not awarded any compensation because the evidence before everyone's eyes was clear that there was no compensation owed (Johnson 2015, 119-20).

There is no comparable account of the young Jesus in the four canonical gospels. The only account of his childhood, discussed above, concerns a visit to the Temple in Jerusalem, where Jesus stays behind while his parents set off for home. This arguably has the same underlying theme as the incident with the young Nanak ensuring that his spiritual practices have no material impact on anyone, but this perhaps stretches the comparison a bit too far.

The apocryphal Gospel of Thomas does record an incident with a clearer parallel. Jesus makes some birds out of clay, but does so on the Sabbath. A man sees him doing so, and regards this as breaking the Sabbath, because making something out of clay is a form of work. The man goes to fetch Joseph, Jesus' father, to rebuke his son for his bad behaviour. But Jesus simply claps his hands, and the clay birds become alive and fly off. There is therefore no evidence of Jesus breaking the Sabbath, and so no possibility of his being rebuked (Gospel of Thomas 2:1-5). There again are resonances with the story of the young Nanak, but also significant differences. Jesus in the Gospel of Thomas comes across as a bit of a smart-alecky child, who knows he can get away with things by disposing of the evidence (apart from the evidence of a much later date of composition, this is probably one reason why the Gospel of Thomas never attained canonical status). By contrast, the young Nanak is moved with compassion, and so asks the Supreme Being to undo the damage his buffaloes have caused. There is a qualitative difference in the two actions; the former is for personal gain only, whilst the latter is for the good of another.

SIXTH TO TENTH MOST POPULAR *SAKHIS*

The Cobra's Shadow[2]

This is an incident that occurred in Nanak's youth, and occurred in fifty-four per cent of the *janam sakhis* in Johnson's sample. He ranks it joint tenth in his list. When he was young, Nanak loved meditating on the divine. He was even in close contact with the divine when he slept. One day he fell asleep under a tree. The leaves of the tree sheltered his face from the sun. As time passed, the sun moved in the sky and so the leaves no longer protected Nanak from the sun's heat. This meant his face was starting to get burnt by the sun.

A cobra crawled close to Nanak. The cobra saw that Nanak's face was exposed to the sun, and he did not want Nanak to get burnt. He saw that Nanak was in close relationship with God and decided that Nanak was holy and so should be served. The cobra spread its hood over Nanak's face, to give him shelter from the heat of the sun.

While the cobra was hovering over Nanak's face, Rai Bular, head of the village came riding by on his horse. Seeing the snake, he assumed it was poised to strike and kill Nanak. He hurried over, ready to protect Nanak from being bitten by the snake. But as he drew closer, Rai Bular realised that Nanak was in a divine sleep and that somehow the cobra seemed to be meditating as well. Rai Bular concluded that this was not actually a dangerous situation at all. The cobra was not attacking Nanak, but protecting him. This confirmed Rai Bular's view that Nanak was a great saint.

There is no comparable story in the four canonical Gospels, of Jesus being protected or helped by any animals. Children's nativity plays often make much of the different animals that may, or may not, have been present at Jesus'

---

2. Account based on https://www.sikhnet.com/stories/audio/nanak-and-cobra, accessed 5th July 2021.

birth. The New Testament accounts do not mention animals at all; even the donkey which Mary supposedly rode to Bethlehem is a later addition. As for the cows and sheep, whilst it is probable there were animals in the space Mary and Joseph took shelter in when Jesus was born, there is no historical record of exactly what animals they were, and no account of them doing anything to support or care for Jesus.

The closest biblical parallel I can think of is an incident in the fourth chapter of the book of Jonah. Jonah was a Hebrew prophet, whom God called to preach to the people of Nineveh. Jonah did not want to fulfil this obligation, and tried to flee in the opposite direction, towards Tarshish. But a storm blew up, and Jonah realised it was sent by God, so ordered the sailors to throw him overboard. Initially they were reluctant to do so, but eventually complied. Once Jonah was in the water, the storm ceased. Jonah was swallowed by a great fish, and in the belly of the fish he repented and consented to go to Nineveh to preach. He was duly returned to the shore and went to Nineveh. Once there, he preached and the people repented. Jonah, still hopeful that destruction might fall on Nineveh, went outside the city to watch for fire from heaven, sent by God. While he waited in the burning hot sun, he complained of the heat, and God provided a vine to grow and shade him. But God then also provided a scorching east wind, which killed the vine. Jonah complained about the death of the plant – and was rebuked by God, who asked him if he is so concerned about the fate of a plant he did not even nurture himself, how much more should God care for Nineveh, with its thousands of inhabitants.

The parallel is not strong but does remind us of the mercy and protection provided by God. The fact that there is no particular parallel is in no way problematic; it serves as a reminder to consider each faith on its own terms and that any comparative scheme is necessarily flawed.

SIXTH TO TENTH MOST POPULAR *SAKHIS*

Work in Dulat Khan's commissariat

The *janam sakhi* which records Nanak's work in Dulat Khan's commissariat also occurred in fifty-four per cent of Johnson's sources, making it joint tenth most popular in his survey. McLeod explains that although by age thirty the Guru was married with two children, his tendency towards renunciation of the material things of life was frustrating his family. Guru Nanak spent all his time talking with holy men, while his parents failed to persuade him to take any interest in commerce or other money-making activities. Eventually, the Guru's brother-in-law, Jai Ram, invited Nanak to join him in Sultanpur. Nanak travelled to Sultanpur, and was interviewed by Daulat Khan, who employed Jai Ram as his steward. Guru Nanak presented Daulat Khan with an Iraqi horse and some money. These gifts pleased Daulat Khan, who ordered Guru Nanak be placed in full authority over his province and his property. Nanak fulfilled his duties diligently, even if his mind was more focused on spiritual matters (1968, 53-54).

The Gospels do not record Jesus' entry into adulthood. After the account of his visit to the temple in Jerusalem aged twelve, Jesus next appears aged thirty and engaged in an itinerant preaching and healing ministry. He is recorded as being a carpenter (or perhaps a builder; in Mark 6:3, Jesus is referred to as the *tekton*, a Greek term that can be translated either way). But he does not have any authoritative position of leadership as Nanak does. There are other figures in the Bible who do rise to authority in this way, notably Joseph and Daniel in the Hebrew Scriptures. But since the focus of this comparison is directly between Jesus and Guru Nanak, I will not discuss those figures here.

Reflections so far

This second set of *sakhis* highlights clearly the differences between Guru Nanak and Jesus; the fact that there are no easy parallels, for example for Nanak's encounter with a cobra reminds us that each followed their own path. There is no value judgement in this observation; rather it is a reminder of the danger of conflating and confusing the story of holy men and women. Each have their own particular message and must be understood and engaged with on their own terms. That is not to say there are no points of connection; the reminder of God's presence everywhere and the importance of love for neighbour, not exploitation of the weak and oppressed remains as relevant to Christians as it does for Sikhs.

Chapter 7

Other Important *Janam Sakhis*

Johnson's survey of the most popular *janam sakhis* is a useful tool for determining which to focus on. But the nature of his lists means that they do not present a chronological account of Guru Nanak's life. In this third discussion of the *janam sakhis*, I will focus on key elements of Nanak's life story that have not yet been discussed, drawing primarily from Johnson's list of other important *sakhis* (that is, those which are eleventh to twentieth most popular). The chapter consists of four main sections: the Guru's birth narrative; further tales of his youth; his marriage and call; and a final section on his discourses with religious leaders during his travels.

OTHER IMPORTANT *JANAM SAKHIS*

Guru Nanak's birth[1]

Guru Nanak was born in 1469 CE in a small village called Talwandi. The village, which is in modern day Pakistan, is now called Nankana, or Nanak's village, in his honour. His mother was Bibi Tripta and his father was Mehta Kalu Ram, known to most people in the village as Kalu Ji. Kalu Ji worked as a *patwari*, keeping records of the land and money expended in the village, which was owned by Rai Bhoe and subsequently by his son Rai Bular, both of whom were converts to Islam.

The first child born to Bibi Tripta and Kalu Ji was a girl, known as Bibi Nanaki. She was at home with her father when the second child, Nanak, was born. A nurse by the name of Daultan attended the birth, and came to tell Kalu Ji the good news that he had a son. But she looked sad when she told him the news. When asked why she explained that normally children cry when they are born, but that this boy had simply smiled.

Kalu Ji was worried that there was something wrong with his son; and asked Daultan if anything else out of the ordinary had happened. She explained that when Nanak was born, a dazzling light, like a star, shone around his head. Wanting to understand what all this meant, Kalu Ji fetched a pandit, a local holy man, called Hardyal. He talked with Daultan and reassured Kalu Ji that all would be well, and that his son would be either a king or a Guru.

Hearing this prediction about her younger brother, Bibi Nanaki spoke up, saying she was sure that he would not be a king. Her father told her to be quiet, asking why she didn't want her brother to be a king. She replied that while she

---

1. Based on https://www.sikhmissionarysociety.org/sms/smspublications/gurunanakforchildren/chapter1/ and http://www.discoversikhism.com/sikh_gurus/guru_nanak_birth_of_a_guru.html Accessed 6th August 2021.

Guru Nanak's birth

would love him to become a king, that would not happen. Rather he would become a Guru, a prediction that did indeed come true.

The stories of Nanak as a baby say he was unusual; he never cried as babies normally do. Even if he was hungry or it was time for his milk, he did not cry. Whenever he slept, his face looked very bright and he seemed to smile. He always had a close bond with his sister; whenever she held him or talked with him, his face would shine with delight.

There is no record in the New Testament as to whether Jesus cried as a baby or not; the traditional carol "Away in a Manger," written in 1882, includes the line "No crying he makes," but this is simply speculation. The New Testament does record that angels announced his birth to shepherds, who subsequently came to visit Jesus. They were told that the baby they were looking for would be in a manger, a feeding trough for animals; an unusual enough fact that it was presumably simple enough to find the correct child (Luke 2:8-20). Subsequently (perhaps a year later), magi(astronomers) came from Persia to also give gifts and worship Jesus (Matthew 2:1-12). Their gifts of gold, frankincense and myrrh are traditionally understood within Christian thought as signs of Jesus' status as both prophet, king and priest, as well as signifying his death, which Christians believe deals with all the sin and failure in the world.

Thus, the birth of both these great and holy men was accompanied by signs and predictions of their future work. There is scope for sceptical debate as to the historicity of these signs, but for the eyes of faith, there is no reason to doubt they occurred. Moreover, the point is that they attest to the holiness of the young child, demonstrating that they were the object of faith-filled devotion from birth.

OTHER IMPORTANT *JANAM SAKHIS*

Further tales of Nanak's youth

This section will examine two further *sakhis*, one concerning instruction of the young Nanak by the Mullah, and the second a visit from a physician when the Guru stopped eating. Both show what an extraordinary young man he was.

Kalu Ji hoped that his firstborn son Nanak would follow in his footsteps at the village *patwari*; as such it was necessary for him to learn Persian and Arabic. Kalu Ji's master, Rai Dular, had promised that Nanak would become Kalu Ji's successor if he mastered the necessary languages and showed all the other requisite skills. Nanak's education was therefore very important in Kalu Ji's eyes. The father took his son to the local Mullah and asked him when would be an auspicious day for his son to start his education. The Mullah consulted his calendar and realised that the next day was the day that the Prophet Muhammad ended his meditation in the Hira cave on the mountain Jabal-an-Nour near Mecca. As such it was a suitable occasion for Nanak to commence his education.

The next morning, when Nanak went to the Mullah to begin his lessons, he took with him some sweets and a silver rupee as an offering to his teacher. The Mullah duly distributed the sweets to some local children and then began writing on his blackboard. He began to teach Nanak the Persian alphabet. He wrote the first ten letters, and asked Nanak to memorise these and return the next day to learn more. But Nanak replied that he had already learnt them, and asked to be shown more. The Mullah duly complied, and Nanak was easily able to memorise the whole Persian alphabet in that first lesson.

Nanak then asked his teacher what the real meaning of these letters was. The Mullah responded that they were sim-

Further tales of Nanak's youth

ply letters. But Nanak went into a divine trance and spoke out the meaning of each letter, as follows:[2]

- ALIF (الف) This word represents the Divine Qalma, Bange Aasmani or Allah. It says that you have to always remember God and banish any neglect of Him from thy heart.

- BE (ب) This word asks you to renounce heresy and walk according to the Shariah. Be humble before every one, and call no one bad.

- TE (ت) This word asks you to repent with sincerity of heart lest you afterwards grieve. Ask for forgiveness from God for your sin and keep your mind in prayer.

- SE (ث) This word asks you to praise God very much; to not draw breath without doing so.

- JIM (ج). One has to earn spiritual wealth by reciting Lord's name and meditation and only that wealth will go after death. You should keep this wealth else agents of death (Kaal) will rob you of wealth of good deeds during your transit after death and then you will be punished for your misdeeds.

- HE (ح) This word asks you to embrace humility, and asks you to renounce the pride of you heart.

- KHE (خ) This word tells that they were kafirs (traitors) who forgot their Creator; their minds were bent on the hoarding of wealth, and they bore loads of sin upon their heads. Real lovers of God always remember God.

- DAL (دال) This word exhorts people to be honest, and to not sleep the whole night through without remembering the

2. Adapted slightly from https://barusahib.org/general/when-guru-nanak-dev-ji-amazed-the-devout-muslim-priest-with-his-knowledge/ Accessed 30th July 2021

OTHER IMPORTANT *JANAM SAKHIS*

Lord. You must awaken, at least for part of the night, for prayer.

- ZAL (ذال) This word asks you to remember God. The remembrance of God will help you to cross the gate of death very easily and devil's agents will not punish you and way to God will be very smooth.

- RE (ر) This word tells you that the advantage of having faith in God is that you will know when you arrive before God. Restrain from the five evil passions (lust, anger, greed, false attachment and egotism), and apply your heart to God.

- ZE (ذ) This word asks you to practise humility, the Lord is independent and does not need anyone's support. It is not through your efforts but His grace that enables you to reach Him. So be humble.

- SIN (سین) This word implores you to search your heart; the Lord is in you. You do not have to go to temple or mosque to search him. You are the highest among His creation and God has bestowed you the privilege of meeting him and whole of this creation is in your service.

- SHIN (شین) This word assures you that you will obtain martyrdom if you die for the love of the dear One. This human body is the temple of living God, the natural mosque where God is calling you every day with his beautiful Azan(prayer call) but you remain sleeping.

- SUAD (صاد) Let your mind be contented when you obtain your allotted food. God arranges food for even insects living inside stones, birds and flowers. Why should you worry about daily bread?

- ZUAD (ضاد) This word reveals that God's splendour and grace is lost for those individuals who associate themselves

Further tales of Nanak's youth

only with worldly affairs. Arise, look before you, and do not immerse yourself completely in the play of the world.

- TOE (طوے) Embrace *tariqat* (walking in God's way) and enter *marafat* (divine knowledge through the perfect master) and finally attain the age of certainty of union with God.

- ZOE (ظوے) This word signifies the misery of tyrants who did not heed the Lord's Name. How can man obtain peace without his Master?

- 'AIN (عن) This word advises people to practice good deeds to the best of their ability. Without good works and virtues people die full of regret.

- GHAIN (غن) This word tells you that those who attain self-realization are rich who know themselves. You will know God only after you know yourself.

- FE (ف) This word signifies that people should do all their duties with this world but keep their minds in God, and think their duties and possessions are not their own.

- QAF (قاف) This word represents those in whose hearts the love of God has arisen; they shall have no rest till they find Him. The bodies of those who have met the Lord God have become refined gold. Those who waste their time in sensual pleasures are likely lowly insect born in vomit and sputum.

- KAF (کاف) This word implores that you should remember your creed; in what else is there profit? You are the soul, a drop in ocean of super-consciousness. You should aspire for merging in the Lord, your true source.

- GAF (گاف) This word explains that man's mind is wanton; if you restrain it, you shall plant your feet firmly on the way to *haqiqat* (realization of union with the divine).

OTHER IMPORTANT *JANAM SAKHIS*

- LAM (لام) This word explains that sufferings will rain on those who abandon their prayers and they lose whatever little or much they have earned by their good deeds. Satan takes them and punishes for their bad deeds.

- MIM (مَ) This word signifies that following the dictates of mind, egotism and wilfulness is prohibited; you should walk as your spiritual guide directs you to.

- NUN (نون) This word emphasises that one should look to truth alone, and know that the world is *maya* (illusion). They who think the world is true shall die confounded.

- WAW (واو) This word stresses that those who associate with the True become *faqirs* (saints). The more they remember God, the more they love Him.

- HE (ح) This word emphasises that you should be in fear of that day when God will judge you. Always do good deeds and spend your time in remembrance of God.

The Mullah was amazed at Nanak's depth of knowledge and insight; he recognised that God was at work in this young child. Nanak soon mastered all the learning that the Mullah set him.

Before too long Nanak had already mastered all the learning that the Mullah and his other teachers had to offer him, so he stopped going to school. But he also refused to join his father's business, preferring to spend his time with saints and holy men. He learnt all that he could from these people, but when there was no one to learn from, Nanak spent his time alone in his room, meditating.

The behaviour worried his parents; Nanak was forgetting to eat and seemed to have no interest in ordinary daily life. They called a doctor to come and check up on Nanak's health. Nanak's parents explained to the doctor that their son was acting strangely, but that they did not know what was wrong with him. The doctor went into Nanak's room and tried to take his pulse on his wrist, but Nanak withdrew his arm, asking the doctor what he was doing.

"I want to take your pulse," the doctor explained. "Once I have heard your heart beat, I can diagnose your illness and then work out what medicine or treatment you need."

Guru Nanak laughed at him. He knew that it was not he who was ill, but other people, who lived in a worldly way, chasing after pleasure and other things. So Guru Nanak spoke the following Shabad:

> They have sent for the physician for me!
> He has taken my hand and felt my pulse.
> What can a pulse disclose?
> The pain lies deep in the heart.
> Physician, go back and heal yourself,
> Diagnose your own disease,
> Then you may diagnose the disease of others,
> And call yourself a physician (AG 1279).[3]

The doctor responded, asking if Nanak thought that he was ill. Guru Nanak replied that he was suffering from a sickness of the soul, the disease of egotism, which separates us from God, the source of life. The doctor then enquired as to whether that was any cure. The Guru replied:

> When man shall possess the Name of the Bright One,
> His body shall become like gold and his soul be made pure;
> All his pain and disease shall be dispelled,

---

3. Taken from http://www.discoversikhism.com/sikh_gurus/guru_nanak_doctor.html. Accessed 30th July 2021

OTHER IMPORTANT *JANAM SAKHIS*

> And he shall be saved, Nanak, by the true Name.
> (AG 1256).[4]

Guru Nanak explained that he and the doctor both suffered from the same sickness; a lack of purity which meant they cannot be close to God. The only difference was that while Guru Nanak knew he was afflicted by this illness, others did not seem to care at all.

The doctor was surprised when he heard such deep wisdom from someone so young. He saw that he had a pure and deep love for God. He reported to Nanak's parents that their son was not ill, he was simply immersed in the love of God and did not need any medicine. Nanak's parents accepted this diagnosis, although they still did not fully understand their own child.

After Jesus was tempted in the desert, he returned to his hometown of Nazareth. He attended synagogue on the Sabbath, as was his custom, and read from the Isaiah scroll, as discussed above. Once he had finished reading, he told the congregation that the scripture had been fulfilled that day in their hearing. The crowd's response was sceptical – isn't this Joseph's son? That is to say, they knew his lineage and so could not accept him as the messenger of God he was now claiming to be. In response to their scepticism, Jesus then said to them,

> Doubtless you will quote to me this proverb, "Doctor, cure yourself!" And you will say, "Do here also in your hometown the things that we have heard you did at Capernaum." (Luke 4:23 NRSV).

---

4. Taken from http://www.discoversikhism.com/sikh_gurus/guru_n anak_doctor.html. Accessed 30th July 2021

There are probably two points being made. First that Jesus must do for them miracles such as those he has done in a neighbouring town, a simple case of local rivalry. Second, that Jesus must back up his verbal claims with actions. Jesus refused to do so, arguing that a prophet is not accepted in his own town, presumably because people do not expect great things of him, having seen him as a child.

This is not quite the same point as that Guru Nanak makes. The Guru is talking to an actual doctor; his point is that this man, who is skilled in the diagnosis of physical ailments needs also to recognise the spiritual malady that burns within his soul. The ultimate point, that all people are in need of spiritual healing and the audience are unable to see that, is common to the two accounts, although the ending is different, for while the doctor recognises Nanak's deep spirituality, the crowd in the Nazareth synagogue are deeply frustrated by Jesus' provocations and try to stone him to death for blasphemy.

The Guru's Marriage and his call[5]

Guru Nanak's father, Kalu Ji, decided that it was time for him to get married, to the daughter of Mool Chand, who was called Bibi Sulakhni. Nanak refused to conform to the cultural expectations of the day, whereby Brahmin priests would select a particularly auspicious day for a wedding ceremony to take place. As far as Guru Nanak was concerned, any day was an auspicious day to get married.

Mool Chand organised a debate between some local Brahmins and the Guru to determine exactly when and how the wedding ceremony should take place. The Guru was sitting

---

5. Based on http://www.discoversikhism.com/sikh_gurus/guru_nanak_marriage.html. Accessed 30th July 2021.

next to a crooked mud wall while this discussion took place. Bibi Sulakhni's family became worried that this wall would fall on the Guru, and asked an elderly lady to warn him of the danger.

Having been duly warned, the Guru simply smiled at her and told her that the wall would not fall for centuries, but the will of God would prevail. The wall is still standing, within Gurdwara Kand Sahib, and a celebration is held there every year on the anniversary of the Guru's marriage.

When Nanak married Sulakhni, he did not follow the expected rituals, circumambulating the sacred fire only four times instead of the expected seven, and making a speech, which has unfortunately not been preserved. The couple had two sons: Sri Change and Lakhmi Das. But marriage did not distract Guru Nanak from his main focus of meditation and proclaiming the teachings he was given by God. For the Guru, the whole of humanity was his family, not merely those he married or fathered.

Jesus did not marry; speculation that he had some form of a relationship with Mary Magdalene is just that, unfounded speculation. Although it was unusual in his context for a man to remain single and celibate, that is what Jesus did. Christianity thus recognises both marriage and celibacy as equally valid choices. The Apostle Paul taught that being single was advantageous for those who wished to focus on the proclamation of the Gospel. Without the distractions and responsibilities of family life, he argued, one has more time to devote to active service of others and preaching the Good News (1 Corinthians 7:1-16). This is not a hard and fast rule for Christians; there is equally no prohibition on marriage. The contrast with the Guru is in marital status; both Jesus and Guru Nanak devoted themselves primarily to the work they felt God had called them to. Moreover, both appear to have defined family more in terms of followers than biological relations. Jesus does this in a particularly striking way. Once, when he was speaking to a crown, his mother, brothers and sisters came to him, and asked for him. But he responded:

> "Who are my mother and my brothers?" And looking at those who sat around him, he said, "Here are my mother and my brothers! Whoever does the will of God is my brother and sister and mother." (Mark 3:33-35, NRSV).

The Guru's travels and discourses

The bulk of the *janam sakhis* consists of accounts of Guru Nanak's travels and discourses with religious and secular leaders. Seven *sakhis*, a small fraction of the total incidents recorded, are discussed in this section. Those discussed here are: instruction by the pandit; discourse with the qazi; the cannibal's cauldron; the sack of Saidpur; Duni Chand's flags; Jagannath Puri; and the discourse on Mount Sumeru. The discussion closes with a reflection on Christian points of connection.

Instruction by the Pandit[6]

This incident took place during 1510, during Guru Nanak's first preaching journey. It concerns an encounter with a Pandit named Kalyug, who was exploiting gullible spiritual seekers. These people would come to Kalyug, who would sit crosslegged before them, often with his eyes closed. He would sometimes close one nostril, and then suddenly declare he

---

6. Based on https://www.allaboutsikhs.com/sikh-youth/guru-sakhis/guru-nanak-and-kaljug-pandit/ Accessed 1st August 2021

was seeing Vishnu in heaven or that he was visiting Brahmpuri, the Dwelling of Brahma, or Shivpurio, the Dwelling of Shiva. His audience were awestruck, and made offerings to him, placing them in a small jug that Kalyug placed before him.

The Pandit Kalyug would ask all those present to also close their eyes while he meditated, claiming it helped his visions. Once, when all had closed their eyes, Guru Nanak ordered Mardana to hide the small jug into which offerings to Kalyug were placed. When the Pandit opened his eyes, he noticed the jug had gone, and flew into a great rage, demanding to know who had hidden it and where they had put it.

Guru Nanak responded, "Pandit, you were able to see the Dwelling of Vishnu, Shiva and Brahma, surely you can also see where your missing jug is lying? How can you see the dwelling place of the gods but not a simple jug?"

But the Pandit could not tell where the jug was hidden, and so his deceit was exposed. He was impressed by Guru Nanak's spiritual insights, and asked him to stay with him. Guru Nanak obliged, and led the Pandit to the true spiritual path.

The Guru is said to have spoken these words to reflect the situation with Kalyug:

> One Universal Creator God. By The Grace Of The True Guru:
> No, no, this is not the time, when people know the way to Yoga and Truth.
> The holy places of worship in the world are polluted, and so the world is drowning.
> In this Dark Age of Kali Yuga, the Lord's Name is the most sublime.
> Some people try to deceive the world by closing their eyes and holding their nostrils closed.

> They close off their nostrils with their fingers,
> and claim to see the three worlds.
> But they cannot even see what is behind them.
> What a strange lotus pose this is!
> The Kshatriyas have abandoned their religion,
> and have adopted a foreign language.
> The whole world has been reduced to the same
> social status; the state of righteousness and
> Dharma has been lost.
> They analyze eight chapters of (Panini's) gram-
> mar and the Puraanas.
> They study the Vedas, but without the Lord's
> Name, no one is liberated;
> So says Nanak, the Lord's slave. (AG 662).

Discourse with the Qazi[7]

This incident took place soon after the Guru had vanished for three days after bathing in the River Bein. When he reappeared he declared that "there is no Hindu, there is no Musulman," a statement that puzzled the local Qazi (Muslim judge), who asked Guru Nanak to explain what he meant. After an initial discussion, the Qazi and Guru Nanak accompanied a local governor, Daulat Khan, to say *namaz* (Muslim prayer). While the two prayed, Guru Nanak watched them, and even laughed at them. This upset the Qazi, who asked the Guru why he was engaged in such rude behaviour. The Guru responded that the Qazi's prayers had not been accepted because his mind was elsewhere, thinking of a new born filly at home, rather than focusing on his prayers. The Qazi admitted that this was indeed the case, thus admitting that the Guru had superior spiritual powers.

---

7. Based on the account in Johnson 2015, 107-8.

OTHER IMPORTANT *JANAM SAKHIS*

The cannibal's cauldron[8]

This episode occurred as Guru Nanak travelled back from a distant journey to East India. Passing through central India, the Guru was ministering to the communities that lived there. His companion Mardana was foraging for food and was seized by a local giant, named Kauda. Kauda was the leader of a clan of cannibals, and always kept a cauldron boiling to cook any man or beast that he captured. Mardana would have met the same fate but for the Guru's timely appearance.

The Guru said "Sat Kartar – the Creator is the eternal truth" by way of greeting to Kauda. The cannibal was startled, and when he turned to see who had spoken, he was touched as never before by the sight of Guru Nanak. He had never seen such calm or tranquillity on a person before. Letting Mardana go, he fell at the Guru's feet, and became a Sikh.

Johnson comments that the power of the Guru's words to bring change is seen in his greeting, "Sat Kartar," which explains that the Divine is both Creator and true; thus truth is the essence of the world. A simple two-word greeting is sufficient; there is no need for lengthy hymns or expositions.

The sack of Saidpur[9]

This concerns the invasion of Punjab by Babar, also known as Zghir ud-Din Mohammad, the founder of the Mughal dynasty of India. He invaded repeatedly through the period 1483-1530, with an army that brought devastation to the region. Guru Nanak's four hymns on the invasions are collectively known as *Babarvani* (Babar's command or sway). Three

---

8. Based on the account in Johnson 2015, 136.
9. Based on https://www.sikhiwiki.org/index.php/Babar\%27s_Invasion. Accessed 1st August 2021

The Guru's travels and discourses

of these are found on pages 360 and 417-18 of the standard editions of the Guru Granth Sahib, and the fourth on pages 722-23.

The first invasion came as far as Peshawar; in the following year he reached Saidpur (now Eminabad in modern day Pakistan), where Guru Nanak was amongst those taken captive. Subsequent invasions brought further havoc and greater conquest for Babar.

The Sikh tradition recalls a meeting between Babar and Guru Nanak that took place in 1520 during the invasion of Saidpur. Nanak was amongst the captives, and was given a load to carry. His companion Mardana was given a horse to lead. But Mir Khan, one of the invaders, saw that the Guru's burden was carried without any support and that Mardana's horse followed him without any reins, for Guru Nanak was at that moment receiving a revelation that Mardana was recording. He reported this to Babar, who is said to have responded that if a holy man had lived in Saidpur, then the town should not have been destroyed.

Babar met with the Guru and kissed his feet, asking the holy man what he should give him. Guru Nanak's response was to ask for nothing for himself, but simply to request that the prisoners of Saidpur be released and their property returned to them. This request was granted.

One of the Guru's hymns within Babarvani indicates the Guru's belief that Babar was sent as an agent of God, to bring punishment on those who had broken God's laws:

> Lord, Thou takest Khurasan under Thy wing,
> but yielded India to the invader's wrath.
> Yet thou takest no blame;
> And sendest the Mughal as the messenger of death.
> When there was such suffering, killing, such shrieking in pain,
> Didst not Thou, O God, feel pity?

OTHER IMPORTANT *JANAM SAKHIS*

The fourth of the Babarvani hymns is probably addressed to Bhal Lalo, who was one of the Guru's devotees and lived in Saidpur. It sets out both the Guru's distress at the violence he witnessed and also his belief in the ultimate victory of God over all forms of evil:

> As descendeth the Lord's word to me, so do I deliver it unto you, O Lalo:
> [Babar] leading a wedding-array of sin hath descended from Kabul and demandeth by force the bride, O Lalo.
> Decency and righteousness have vanished, and falsehood struts abroad, O Lalo.
> Gone are the days of Qazis and Brahmans, Satan now conducts the nuptials, O Lalo.
> The Muslim women recite the Qur'an and in distress remember their God, O Lalo.
> Similar is the fate of Hindu women of castes high and low, O Lalo.
> They sing paeans of blood, O Nanak,
> and by blood, not saffron, ointment is made, O Lalo.
> In this city of corpses, Nanak proclaimeth God's praises, and uttereth this true saying:
> The Lord who created men and put them to their tasks watcheth them from
> His seclusion.
> True is that Lord, true His verdict, and true is the justice He dealeth.
> As her body's vesture is torn to shreds, India shall remember my words.
> In seventy-eight they come, in ninety seven shall depart; another man of
> destiny shall arise.
> Nanak pronounceth words of truth, Truth he uttereth; truth the time calls for.

The reference to seventy-eight and ninety-seven probably refers to 1578 and 1597 in the Indian calendar, which indicates 1521 and 1540 in the Gregorian calendar, the dates of Babar's invasion and the dethronement of his son Hayuman by Sher Khan. There is thus a mix of historically specific prophecy and general teaching and lament within this hymn.

Duni Chand's flags[10]

This story concerns a challenge that Guru Nanak issued to a wealthy man named Duni Chand, namely whether he could take a needle with him into the afterlife. Duni Chand recognises that this is not possible, and asks the Guru what he should do. He is instructed to give away his wealth to the poor and needy for he did not earn it through honest means. The only wealth one can expect to take into the afterlife is that earned through one's own honest labour and what one gives away in charity. Johnson subsequently comments that the focus of this particular *sakhi* is on encouraging *seva*, or selfless service of others (2015, 196-97).

Mention of wealth and needles brings to mind the story of the rich young man, already mentioned above. In Mark (10:17-27) and Matthew (19:16-22) he is rich and young, whilst in Luke (18:18-25) he is merely a "certain ruler." In each account, he comes to Jesus, asking what he should do to inherit eternal life. Jesus' initial response is to ask whether he has kept the commandments, to not murder, steal or commit adultery, to honour one's parents and to love one's neighbour as oneself. The man replies that he has kept all these commands since his youth. Jesus then sets out one final condition: he must give his wealth to the poor. This is a challenge too far for the man, who goes away sad, and presumably does not rise to the request. Jesus comments that it

---

10. Based on Johnson 2015, 186.

is easier for a camel to go through the eye of a needle than for a rich person to enter the Kingdom of God (Matthew 19:23; Mark 10:25; Luke 18:25). Whilst some interpreters conjure up fantasies about a gate into Jerusalem called the "needle gate" that a camel could squeeze through if all its burdens are removed, this completely misses the point. Jesus is telling a joke. The hyperbole of an enormous camel and a tiny eye of a needle makes the fairly obvious point that if you rely on your wealth to get what you want and need, you're unlikely to rely on God for what you really need, namely salvation that is his gift alone.

Jagan Nath Puri[11]

The incident at the temple of Jagan Nath took place not long after that involving the cannibal's cauldron. The Guru was returning back towards his hometown, but stopped at the temple of Jagan Nath, one of the four most revered holy sites in Hinduism. The statue of Jagan Nath was reputed to have been carved by the architect of the gods, and installed by Lord Brahma himself. It was evening when the Guru arrived at the temple, and the priests were conducting Arti, offering their worship to Jagan Nath.

Although the Guru was invited to join in, he declined. When asked why, he explained that at that very moment a far more beautiful offering of worship was being offered by nature before the invisible altar of the divine. At this worship, the sun and moon were the lamps, the firmament was the salver that supported them and the fragrance from the Malayan mountains was the incense. The Guru then spoke this Sikh shabad of Arti:

11. Based on http://www.discoversikhism.com/sikh_gurus/guru_n anak_jagannath_puri.html. See also https://www.allaboutsikh s.com/sikh-youth/guru-sakhis/guru-nanak-in-jaganath-puri-aarti/. Accessed 2nd August 2021.

The Guru's travels and discourses

The sun and moon, O Lord, are thy lamps; the firmament
Thy salver; the orbs of the stars, the pearls enchased in it.
The perfume of the sandal is Thine incense; the wind is thy fan;
All the forests are Thy flowers, O Lord of light.
What worship is this, O Thou Destroyer of birth?

Unbeaten strains of ecstasy are the trumpets of Thy worship.
Thou hast a thousand eyes and yet not one eye;
Thou hast a thousand forms and yet not one form;
Thou hast a thousand pure feet and yet not one foot;
Thou hast a thousand organs of smell and yet not one organ-
I am fascinated by this play of Thine.
The Light which is in everything is Thine, O Lord of Light.
From its brilliancy everything is brilliant;
By the Guru's teaching the light becometh manifest.
What pleaseth Thee is the real Arti.
O God, my mind is fascinated with Thy lotus feet as the
bumble-bee with the flower: night and day I thirst for them.
Give the water of Thy grace to the sarang Nanak, so that he may dwell in Thy name. (AG 663).

OTHER IMPORTANT JANAM SAKHIS

Mount Sumeru[12]

The account of the discourse between Guru Nanak and the Sidhs (proven yogic masters) on Mount Sumeru is a further example of the core teaching of the corruption of religion. Nanak is challenged as to his identity and reason for coming to Mount Sumeru, but responds by saying that the world is in darkness and that no one is seeking out the truth. The disciples of the Sidhs are in the world but have little or no impact; whilst they know how to smear their bodies in ash and beg for food, they are unable to provide spiritual guidance. They put on performances, asking for alms and distribute good luck charms, but do nothing of real spiritual importance. Equally the Mullahs of Islam are corrupt, taking bribes and no longer dispensing justice.

The Sidhs then challenge Guru Nanak as to whether he is a householder or a renunciant. But the Guru's response is that they have misunderstood these terms. One who is a householder is not one who is absorbed in mundane, day-to-day matters, but rather one who earns money honestly, shares his wealth generously and is immersed completely into love of the divine. There is no relevance to whether one lives with one's family or not. The question is whether one is detached from the desires of this world. One should focus primarily on active service of others; religious practices such as chanting and prayer are also important to aid detachment, but one must care for those in need and not isolate oneself completely from the world.

Christian reflection on the Guru's travels and discourses

Reading these *sakhis* that discuss the Guru's travels and encounters with religious leaders, especially the encounter at

---

12. Summarised from https://sikhri.org/articles/guru-nanak-sahi b-the-sidhs-inni-kaur. Accessed 2nd August 2021.

the temple of Jagan Nath and on Mount Sumeru, I was struck primarily by the contrast with Christianity. Jesus does regularly expose religious hypocrisy, and argues against outward piety that has no inner substance as its foundation, not least in his Sermon on the Mount (Matthew 5-7). In these three chapters Jesus intensifies and goes to the heart of the Mosaic Law, demanding not simply outward conformity to the divine standard, but complete inner orientation of the heart towards the way God wants us to live. To give but two examples, calling someone a fool is as bad as murder and looking at another with lust is the same as committing adultery. But Jesus does not really engage with religious charlatans or crooks; his argument is primarily with those in positions of spiritual authority. There is, perhaps, a slight resonance with the discourse with the Qazi, in that Jesus insists that the outward status of a leader must be matched by an inner piety and devotion that is not open to question or rebuke.

I can think of no obvious point of connection with the encounter with a cannibal. It is not really a parallel at all, but it is noticeable that Jesus is content to care for the needs of those regarded by many of his Jewish contemporaries as enemies, whether it is in healing the servant of a Centurion (Luke 7:1-10; Matthew 8:5-13), healing a Syrophoenician woman's daughter (Mark 7:24-30; Matthew 15:21-28) or engaging in religious discourse with a Samaritan woman (John 4). Equally, Jesus never experienced military invasion or conquest, although he arguably did predict the siege and destruction of Jerusalem in 70 CE (Mark 13; Matthew 24). It is striking that Guru Nanak survives the siege of Saidpur, indeed that he is recognised as a great religious teacher, and so honoured with his freedom. By contrast, Jesus willingly submits to the Roman authorities, who crucify him. Even John, whose Gospel account portrays Jesus as being entirely in control of his own destiny (John 18:1-6) still has Jesus beaten and mocked by the Roman soldiers before they crucify him (John 19:1-2). This is the biggest contrast between Sikhi and Christianity; the Guru does die, but his death has no salvific value. Jesus' death, on the other hand, is the culmination and purpose of his life. The whole point is that he came to die; escaping death was a possibility (when the disciples were all asleep in Gethsemane, there was little to stop Jesus from fleeing into the desert other than his own determination to stay). But that possibility never transpired. While the Guru's life is the inspiration for Sikhs, it is in Jesus' death that a Christian finds salvation and life.

Chapter 8

Conversations between Christians and Sikhs

This chapter discusses three areas; the founding of the faiths; John Parry's *The Word of God is not bound*; and Gopal Singh's *The Man Who Never Died*.

The founding of the faiths

One fruitful area of dialogue is the circumstances in which the different faiths were founded. The circumstances for Christianity and Sikhi are really quite different.

It is hard to say when Christianity began. Was it when Jesus was born? When he began his public teaching ministry? When he rose from the dead? When Gentiles (those who are not Jewish) became followers of Jesus? When Christianity became the religion of the Roman Empire? Certainly not the first alternative; Jesus did not teach at birth. Nor the last; Christianity was already established as a faith by this time. Whilst this much is clear, identifying a "place where it all began" is hard, although the events in Jerusalem from Jesus' triumphal entry, through the Last Supper, his crucifixion, resurrection and ascension and the gift of the Holy Spirit to the first followers of Jesus are probably the strongest contender for the "birthday" of the Christian faith. This period, of less than two months, is the formative moment from which the Christian Church emerged.

The main events are as follows. Jesus rode in to Jerusalem on a donkey; his followers waved palm branches and sang songs of praise to God. The whole scene echoed the triumphal entry of Judas Maccabeus several centuries before, hinting that Jesus was claiming identity as a redeemer and rescuer of God's people. The day after he arrived, Jesus went to the Jerusalem temple, and scattered the money changers and animal sellers' tables. A few days later, he shared a meal, perhaps a Passover Meal, with his followers, and instituted the ritual that has now become Holy Communion or the Eucharist. That night he was arrested, tried before the Jewish and Roman authorities and sentenced to death by crucifixion. He was crucified and buried hastily on the Friday, known now as "Good Friday," and buried in a borrowed tomb. The following Sunday, when some of his followers went to administer proper burial rites, the tomb was empty. Jesus then appeared to his followers over a period of forty days, teaching and encouraging them, before ascending to heaven. His followers then had to wait in Jerusalem for ten days. On Pentecost, fifty days after Easter Sunday, they received the gift of the Holy Spirit, and began to spread the message of Jesus throughout the world.

The Khalsa was founded at Anandpur during Vaisakhi 1699. Before giving an overview of what took place, Cole is

The founding of the faiths

clear that not all the historical details of this momentous occasion has been preserved. Whilst that may be true, Guru Gobind Rai, the tenth leader of the Sikhs (who later became known as Guru Gobind Singh), summoned his followers to a gathering to deal with issues of morale and leadership. Up until this time, authority was delegated to the *massands* (missionary messengers), but this system was no longer functioning properly.

During the gathering, the Guru emerged from his tent, holding a drawn sword. He demanded that a Sikh offer his head to the Guru. No one responded, all standing in shocked silence until eventually a Sikh named Daya Ram came forward, following the Guru into the tent. A thud was heard, and the Guru appeared alone, blood dripping from his sword. The Guru repeated his request, and a second man, Dharam Das came forward. There was another thud and the Guru appeared for a third time. This time the volunteer was Mukhand Chand. Two more demands were made and Himman Rai and Sahib Chand offered themselves.

After the fifth time, the Guru opened his tent. All five men were standing there, unharmed, next to the bodies of five decapitated goats. The total dedication of these five Sikhs to their Guru was seen as the moment of renewal for the faith (hence Jakobsh (2012, 35) describes the five volunteers as *Daya* (Compassion); *Dharm* (Duty); *Muhkam* (Firmness); *Himmat* (Effort), and *Sahib* (Honour)). The Guru and his five loyal followers sat together as he addressed the crowd, saying:

In the time of Guru Nanak there was found one devout Sikh, namely Guru Angad. In my time there are found five Sikhs totally devoted to the Guru. These shall lay anew the foundations of Sikhism and the true religion shall become current and famous throughout the world (Cole 1982, 69).

The whole gathering prostrated themselves in front of the six Sikhs seated before them, committing themselves afresh to follow the Guru's teaching. Guru Gobind Rai then took some sugar crystals and dissolved them in water, which was in an iron bowl. He stirred the bowl with a double-edged sword as he recited Guru Nanak's *Japji*, the *Jap* he himself had composed, the *Anand* of Guru Amar Das and *Chaupai*. This liquid, *amrit*, was then given to the five men to drink and sprinkled on their hair and eyes. The Guru then told them to repeat these words:

> Waheguru ji ka Khalsa
> Waheguru ji ki fateh
>
> The Khalsa are the chosen of God,
> Victory be to our God. (Cole 1982, 69)

The five men were then instructed to administer *amrit* to their Guru, by saying:

> I am the son of the Immortal God. It is by his order that I have been born and have established this form of initiation. They who accept it shall henceforth be known as the Khalsa. The Khalsa is the Guru and the Guru is the Khalsa. There is no difference between you and me. As Guru Nanak seated Guru Angad on the throne, so I have made you also a Guru. Wherefore administer the amrit to me without hesitation (Cole 1982, 70).

A strict code of behaviour was established for those initiated into the Khalsa. They were to raise early every morning, to sing the prescribed hymns. They must abandon all other scriptures and sacred texts, nor could they worship any other deities. Those who had taken *amrit* were forbidden from drinking alcohol, taking drugs, or smoking, from sexual relations with Muslim women or eating meat from animals killed according to Muslim rituals (that is, halal meat). Nor could they marry into a family that practised female infanticide. Initiated Sikhs were forbidden to cut their hair. They were to adhere to the five Ks. Men who were admitted took the name Singh, meaning lion and women the name Kaur, which means princess. Thus, Guru Gobind Rai became Guru Gobind Singh.

Cole concludes his discussion by recounting a legend that states that as Guru Gobind Singh was explaining all this to the gathering, two sparrows dipped their beaks into the nectar. They drank some of the liquid and then flew off. As they flew, they confronted and killed a hawk, which is the origin of the Sikh proverb "Through entering the Khalsa, sparrows become hawks." Cole argues that the creation of the Khalsa gave Sikhi a much clearer boundary and its members a sense of pride and purpose. The result is the distinctive body of faith that is easily identified today. Of course, there have been difficulties and debates, for example as to whether a Sikh can run a shop that sells alcohol, but overall the formation of the Khalsa was crucial for the continuation of the faith founded by Guru Nanak (Cole 1982, 67-72).

The Word of God is not Bound

In his survey of the history of dialogue between Sikhs and Christians in the UK, John Parry explains that the first bilateral encounter took place in the autumn of 1984, involving thirty-six people of both faiths. The Christians were members of the United Reformed Church, but the URC never claimed any kind of exclusive rights to the dialogue. A further meeting took place in August 1995, in which the Lord's Prayer and the *mul mantar* were discussed. But the decision to focus on scripture created a further difficulty, as no clear and accurate English translation of the Guru Granth Sahib was available; to overcome this problem, two members of the group would offer a draft translation, which was corrected as the discussion progressed.

Parry explains the methodology used. Each time a theme was chosen, and a passage from the Bible and the Guru Granth Sahib were selected, to be read in turn. If the passage being looked at was from the Sikh scriptures, then the first person to speak was a Christian, and vice-versa, with a Sikh speaking first when the Christian text was discussed. Parry argues this meant everyone was empowered to share what they thought, without fear of offending someone by giving an "incorrect" interpretation. An example of the fruit of their discussions is given in the "monkey hold" versus "cat hold" theories of divine grace. According to Parry, the Sikhs present at the bilateral discussion explained that in north India, many hold to the "monkey hold" doctrine of grace. Just as a baby monkey runs to its mother seeking protection when danger threatens, so human beings must run to God to seek divine grace. By contrast, Christians argued for a "cat hold" doctrine; just as a mother cat seizes a kitten by the scruff of the neck to remove it from danger, so God takes the initiative in searching for his people, whether they deserve his grace or not.

Parry also outlines some of the questions Sikhs brought to the discussion of the Lord's Prayer. I will note five points here. First, reference to God as "father" raised questions, as the Sikhs felt it was an inadequate mode of address; God is both father and mother, as well as friend, guardian and more. Second, the hallowing of God's name was felt to be positive; resonating with the Sikh idea of *Nam Simran*, repeating the divine name as a means of reducing one's self-centredness. Third, questions were raised over what it means for God to have a kingdom, a word that was heard as having too worldly a connotation; God should rule over all creation. Fourth, prayer for "daily bread" was perplexing. God is abundantly generous, so why was this prayer needed? After all, in a Sikh context, the institution of *langar* means food is available to all, as God's gifts are mediated to his people through the *seva* of his servants. Finally, there are Sikh prayers for forgiveness of sins just as there are Christian ones. Parry gives an example:

> *O Lord, our sins are as many as the waters of the ocean, have mercy on us, show us your grace and lead us not into temptation* (Parry 2009, 98).

The picture Parry paints is of an open and productive dialogue, where people both celebrated similarities and disagreed amiably over differences. Other topics covered included debating who Jesus of Nazareth was. Whilst the Sikhs did not recognise him as the incarnation of God, they nevertheless revered him as a teacher whose words and actions had a significant influence on humanity. Furthermore, Jesus' death made Sikhs think of the martyrdoms of Gurus Arjan and Tegh Bahadur. The question of exclusivism was also raised, and the wide variety of Christian positions on the status of Jesus Christ in terms of access to salvation was also explored. Whilst the doctrine of (original) sin does not quite fit with Sikh perspectives on humanity, there are points of contact with the belief that human beings are dominated by *haumai* (pride, self-centredness) from which they need liberation. Similarly, the notion of taking up one's cross daily resonated with Sikh dedication to *seva* for the good of humanity. Faith, the Sikhs added, was expressed in the "game of love," and so life should be characterised by light-heartedness and joy. That does not mean everything is easy. The Sikhs explained that one must walk the "path" of obedience to God, a path that leads to the individual soul merging with the supreme soul. One must set aside personal ambition and pretentiousness, giving up on words and intellectual speculation about the divine in order to enter into true relationship. The final topic Parry outlines is public opinion. A devout Sikh is conspicuous, and so Sikhs learn to be confident in how they live out their faith in their daily lives. Parry suggests the parallel for Christians is not street evangelism but in demanding justice; for Protestants to protest again.

The dialogues did not result in conversion in the sense of Sikhs becoming Christian or vice-versa, but Parry contends that all were converted in the sense of developing new insights, into their own faith as well as the faith of their dialogue partners. For some this was an uncomfortable experience, seeing those who were not Christian exhibit a devotion to God and a lifestyle that many Christians aspire towards. For others it was a welcome challenge, opening up the possibility of further questions and deeper learning. He concludes that first, scripture study was a useful way in to dialogue, especially where original languages were used. Second, that personal faith is enhanced through dialogue both because one is forced to articulate what one actually believes and second because those who come to one's own sacred texts with fresh eyes bring new insights. Third, there is a challenge, in discovering that others also have a profound and deep faith which has no connection with Christianity. What does it mean to talk with someone who is pious and lives a holy life, but has no relationship with Jesus? (Parry 2009, 94-104).

Parry is clear as to the irrelevance of Christianity for Sikhs:

> Sikhism is an autonomous structure which does not need the Christian Church for the fulfilment of its salvific purposes. Therefore any understanding of the Christ figure or possible interpretation using Sikh concepts and values remains simply that—an interpretation. Nor from a Sikh perspective does an appreciation of the Christ figure by a Sikh imply that the Church may be an agent of liberation or salvation (2009, 108).

The Word of God is not Bound

At one level, I agree entirely with Parry; there is no connection between Sikhi and Christianity in the way there is a connection between Christianity and Judaism or even Christianity and Islam. Moreover, any interpretation of Christ from a Sikh perspective is just that, a particular person's perspective. I will doubtless learn from hearing that perspective, attaining fresh insights or discovering why I disagree with what I hear. My understanding of Christian faith resonates more with Abraham Kuyper, who is reported to have said that there is no part of the universe over which Christ does not claim ownership; that is to say, while Sikhs may not think Jesus is of any relevance to them, I personally think he is of complete relevance to them as to everyone, whilst also completely respecting their right to believe me to be mistaken.

That does not mean I presume God is not at work in the lives of Sikhs, nor does it mean I do not have much to learn about my own faith through talking with Sikh friends and colleagues. As noted above, there are many Sikhs whose piety and selflessness is a challenge to half-hearted attempts at Christian discipleship. The Holy Spirit is active beyond the Church, and that includes in the lives of many Sikhs. There is much that can be learnt about Christianity by talking with Sikhs, doing so with gentleness and respect (1 Peter 3:16).

Parry outlines his thoughts on how his Christian faith was impacted by dialogue with Sikh colleagues. He begins by reiterating the points made above, namely that the Sikh concept of *haumai* challenges Christian understandings of individual salvation, and Sikh ease with calling God both Father and Mother challenges the overly gendered understanding of God held by many Christians. His third point concerns *seva*, arguing that a life shaped by the Cross of Christ is a life full of *seva*. He then makes eight further points.

First, that consideration should be given to understandings of atonement and suffering. For a Sikh martyrdom is not passive; hence Parry proposes that the model of *Christus Victor*, the victorious Christ triumphing over death and the devil, is a suitable point from which to begin talking. Second, the nature of humanity and of the human need for redemption. Whilst Christians talk of sin, Sikhs focus more on ignorance, believing people to be unaware of the nature of their relationship with the divine. Third, the understanding of incarnation. Parry argues Sikhs recognise that God is present amongst God's gathered people, which stands in clear contrast with Christian belief in the uniqueness of Christ's incarnation. Fourth, the concept of the Word in both faiths is a fruitful area for dialogue. Parry frames this as an exercise in contrasting *shabad* with *logos*. Fifth, what it means to be a person of faith, what the life of a disciple is like, what it means to seek to deepen one's faith and what costs this entails. Sixth, Parry invites exploration of a spirituality that both dives into the mystery of the divine but also remains rooted in the suffering and pain of the world, seeking justice and recompense for the oppressed and suffering. Seventh, a more nuanced understanding of grace; both Sikhs and Christians recognise that ultimately it is God who fulfils human needs but disagree as to whether it is God or humanity that takes the initiative. Eighth, what does it mean to be a visible person of faith? Devout Sikhs are more easily identified than devout Christians; what do these differences have to teach us about living a life of faith? (Parry 2009, 108-12).

Parry surveys some Sikh responses to Christianity and Christian explanations of Sikhi. Tellingly, he entitles one chapter on the topic "suspicion and concern," which summarises accurately how Sikhs responded. The first Christian missionaries to India had little or no respect for the faith traditions of those they encountered. Whilst many of them were gifted linguists and scholars, they were not empathetic or respectful, but presumed the supremacy of Christianity was a given. Subsequent scholars were trained in the sceptical methods of historical and redaction criticism, and subjected the Guru Granth Sahib to the same type of enquiry that the Bible had been faced with. All this means that many Sikhs were – and remain – suspicious of Christians who want to engage in dialogue. The legacy of empire and colonialism is always in the background of any encounter between white British Christians (such as myself) and Sikhs, even those who were born and raised in Britain. It would be as well for Christians to recognise this and address the concerns early on in any dialogical encounter (2009,116-40).

Parry also provides his personal approach to presenting Christianity to Sikhs. He explains he begins, not with Jesus or God, but with the human condition. Emulating a Buddhist approach to the big questions of life, he points out that "many people seem to be alienated, from others, from their environment, from themselves and from God" (2009, 242). This can be seen in how they treat others, reflecting the truth of Guru Nanak's teaching that people are fundamentally self-centred. This is the second key point Parry makes, that whilst some self-respect and a sense of personal worth is important, this can become over-developed to the detriment of others. Whilst Christians might describe this as sin (not least because of the concept of sin as a human being curved inwards on themselves), Parry focuses instead on self-centredness, whilst recognising that sin is not simply an individualistic concept.

His third point is that this self-centredness must be overcome. For Sikhs, this is encapsulated in the desire to let go of *haumai*, of the ego, the "I" which dominates. Parry cites Luke 9:23, where Jesus commands his followers to take up their cross daily and die to self. This brings out Parry's fourth point, that for a Christian, Jesus is the ultimate example of one who gave himself up for others, most clearly through his death on the cross. But Parry does not believe the Cross of Christ is the be-all and end-all of the situation. Rather he sees it as the start, as for a Christian "living out the cross event on one's own life is the vital, and horrendously difficult, challenge to real faith" (2009, 243). But it is only by giving oneself up in this way that one can find true fulfilment.

Fifth, Parry is clear that one can only live such a surrendered life through the mercy and grace of God. He returns to his point about the initiative of grace; that for a Christian it is God who took the first step, whilst for Sikhs it is a human who must move first. He quotes Bhai Gurdas' teaching that if a person takes a single step towards God, God takes a thousand steps towards that person, and concludes that wherever the initiative comes from, Sikhs and Christians agree that grace is required. Those who live in this way may, to use a Sikh phrase, be *jivan mukhat*, that is have gained liberation, a concept that Parry finds compatible with the notion of being "in Christ." Alternatively, it may be that the believer is following God's *hukam*, God's will, a notion that is relevant for both Sikhs and Christians. But this faith cannot be passive; it must be active, struggling for peace, justice, forgiveness, transformation. Parry quotes a challenge from a Sikh friend, who asked, in the words of Guru Nanak, "What use is your spirituality if my stomach is still empty?" (2009, 243).

As the dialogue deepens, some of the foundational assumptions become more open to question. Parry recognises that "God" is a Christian concept, and Sikhs prefer to speak of "*Akal Purakh*, the Being Beyond Time, the Timeless One, the Eternal" (2009, 244). The doctrine of the Trinity becomes a sticking point for dialogue here, especially since the Guru Granth Sahib begins with "One." Christians and Sikhs have much to talk about when they talk about their belief in the divine. Parry suggests the best way in is to discuss personal experience, which he argues sometimes arises from our relationships with people, whether individually or corporately. This avoids getting too distracted by abstraction and focuses instead on lived experience. As an aside, he notes that Sikhs have addressed Akal Purakh as Mother for hundreds of years;

what is relatively recent within some Christian circles, is long established for Sikhs.

Further topics of discussion are the person and teaching of Jesus, noting that many Sikhs see connections with the martyrdoms of Gurus Arjan and Tegh Bahadur. But the concept of substitutionary atonement, or of propitiation of God's righteous anger against sin has no equivalence within the Sikh faith. Parry also explains he personally finds it unconvincing, accepting the metaphor of ransom if the focus is on liberation and freedom, rather than on to whom the ransom was paid, or the idea of Christ as victor over evil, again provided the focus is personal not cosmic (2009, 247). Christians have a range of views on what are the best metaphors for explaining the work of Christ on the Cross; personally, I find those which Parry has questions about remain useful for me as ways of helping make sense of what Jesus has done for me and for the whole of creation.

Parry's final area of discussion is the faith community. A contrast of the *Khalsa* with the Body of Christ would be a stimulating and enriching conversation. Sikhs recognise the presence of the divine amongst the gathered faithful; Christians believe that when they gather in Christ's name, he is present with them. Both the *Khalsa* and the Body of Christ are centred on what they hold to be the word of God, the Guru Granth Sahib and the Bible respectively. Parry recalls a conversation with a Sikh colleague in which he outlined the concerns of the reformers: *sola gratia* (by grace alone); *sola fide* (by faith alone); *soli deo Gloria* (to the glory of God alone); *sola scriptura* (through the scriptures alone); and *ecclesia reformata semper reformanda* (the Reformed Church must keep on reforming). His colleague responded that these were also the concerns of the Sikhs (2009, 248).

Sikhs and Christians have much to talk about, and many aspects of their lived religious experience have remarkable commonalities and overlaps. There are also clear differences, which are to be celebrated and used to challenge each other to an authentic and active expression of faith. In what follows I will consider a further exploration; the writing of Dr Gopal Singh *The Man Who Never Died*, which is a *bhakti* style meditation of the death and resurrection of Jesus.

The Man Who Never Died

Reading *The Man Who Never Died* is both fascinating and challenging. It presents a portrait of Christ that I recognise in places but do not agree with in others. It weaves theology and history from a unique, Sikh-inspired perspective to paint a portrait of Christ that is both compelling and alive, familiar but also strange. I will discuss three points that speak particularly to the possibility of dialogue between Christians and Sikhs.

First, the way in which Christian teachings are given a particular flavour. For example, Gopal Singh writes

> Men said unto Him
> "How shall we live?"
>
> And He said:
> "By dying to yourselves!"
>
> When asked, "How shall we die?"
> He said: - "By being alive to what never dies within you!" (1990, 6).

This is undoubtedly a reference to Jesus' teaching that to follow him means taking up one's cross and dying daily to self, surrendering control to Christ (Luke 9:23). While I recognise the teaching, I would not have framed it in this way; the reference to that which is within me but never dies is intriguing to contemplate as a way of describing the mutual indwelling of Christ and the believer (John 15:4). I'm not sure this is what Gopal Singh had in mind where he wrote, but it is one place my mind took me.

Another example is the teaching on prayer. In response to a question about how to pray, Gopal Singh has Jesus say:

> Does the seed ask: how shall I pray?
> It enters into its closet, shuts its door,
> and prays in secret as if not praying,
> and fasts as if not fasting, till
> it grows into a flower, and prays
> now with words, but through fragrance (1990, 26).

The echoes of the instructions in the Sermon on the Mount are plain. Jesus is clear that praying in secret is required (Matthew 6:5-6). Equally, one should not worry about the troubles of this life; the flowers are clothed in greater splendour than Solomon, so why worry about clothes (Matthew 6:28-30). From there it is a simple step to prayer as fragrance, not least when incense is known to be the prayers of the saints (Revelation 5:8).

In a productive and open dialogue context, honest reflection on how the other's faith is heard, is both rewarding and challenging. Gopal Singh's writing is an excellent model of this approach. A further reflection on prayer is provocative:

> Prayer is a secret dialogue between lovers, where the mind questions in doubt, and the heart answers in faith (1990, 28).

There is a strong Christian tradition of interpreting the Song of Solomon as an allegory of Christ's relationship with the Church. This understanding of the lover and his beloved is echoed in Revelation, where the new Jerusalem is described as a bride descending in splendour to the wedding feast of the Lamb (Revelation 19:7; 21:2, 9). If this metaphor is extended to the prayer life both of the individual Christian and of the gathered Church, then intercession might be understood as the secret dialogue of lovers. Certainly Christians are encouraged to share their deepest thoughts and desires in their personal prayers, much as one might share one's thoughts with one's spouse.

Second, there are times when Sikh thinking comes to the fore. For example, in reference to Parry's point about the synergies between the death of Jesus and the martyrdoms of Gurus Arjan and Teġh Bhadur, Gopal Singh also utilises themes of martyrdom:

> Upon the pages of tyranny, who is it
> that has scattered across, time and again,
> the molten calligraphy of
> the martyr's blood? (1990, 33).

Whilst it is true that Tertullian is reputed to have described the blood of Christian martyrs as the seed of the church, the idea of "molten calligraphy" speaks more strongly to the Sikh focus on the Guru Granth Sahib as the living Guru, than it does to any Christian notions of martyrdom.

Elsewhere, the Sikh notion of the individual soul attaining union with the divine appears to lie behind some words attributed to Jesus at the Last Supper:

> For, my God is not the God of the dead, but of the living.
> He who loses his life like a drop in the ocean, becomes the ocean himself.
> But, whosoever saves his life from the sea shall lose it in the dust (1990, 53).

Whilst Jesus does describe God as of the living not the dead in his argument with the Sadducees about the resurrection(Mark 12:27; Luke 20:38), there is no sense in that conversation, or elsewhere in the Gospels, that the goal is to attain unity with the divine in the sense of becoming part of the ocean of God. Whilst, as noted above, there is an expectation of mutual indwelling between God and the believer, this is never at the expense of individual corporeal existence. The Christian teaching of the resurrection of the dead presumes we will remain identifiably ourselves post-mortem.

Third, I found reading *The Man Who Never Died* to be an enriching experience, which made helped me see the Gospel stories in a different light. That light was interesting, but I am not sure it always accurately reflected the teaching of the passage on which it was based. In Gopal Singh's retelling of the encounter between Jesus and the Samaritan woman at a well, Jesus speaks in an allegory:

> "Nay, nay," He chastised her, "you've had five husbands – Ego, Wrath, Envy, Infatuation and Greed.
> But now what you live with – Time – is not your husband (1990, 24).

For me, this short extract encapsulates the two points made above. The story comes to life in a different way; describing the woman's five husbands as the five key vices that Guru Nanak identified is innovative and striking. But at the same time, it is a departure from Christian faith. Whilst I found the image interesting, and while it opened up fresh thoughts for me, I cannot read it as the main point of John 4. The focus of that conversation is primarily that God can be worshipped anywhere, without concern for rituals or sacred spaces, provided the worshipper comes through faith in Jesus. The main point to take from this, of course, is that my reading of Sikh texts is biased by my Christian faith. I doubtless bring all sorts of (un)conscious biases to the conversation. I need to recognise this limitation, and where my thoughts are inaccurate or where I misunderstand, be open to correction and challenge.

Chapter 9

Sikhism and Christianity: A Comparative Study

This chapter engages at length with the joint project of Owen Cole and Piara Singh Sambhi (1993), in which they compare and contrast Christianity and Sikhi. In their introduction, Cole and Sambhi list seven basic similarities and one key difference between Sikhi and Christianity. First, that both are "derived religions," in the sense that they developed from another tradition (Hinduism and Judaism respectively). Thus, both Sikhi and Christianity needed to develop a distinct identity; but whilst Judaism rejects Christianity, the same is not true for Hindus and Sikhi. Indeed, Sikhi is not recognised as a distinct faith in India, but is classified by the Constitution as a branch of Hinduism. Second, each claim a distinctive revelation from God, in both cases constituting a protest movement against ritualism and overly formal approaches to religion. Third, a focus on history. The historical Jesus is important to Christians, as the history of the ten Gurus is important to Sikhs. Fourth, both faiths have a collective focus; Christians gather for fellowship in Church, Sikhs are members of the *Panth*, the community that follows the way to liberation taught by Guru Nanak and his successors. Fifth, both faiths take scripture seriously, whether by expecting the Guru Granth Sahib to be present at all religious occasions except for a funeral, or the Christian use of the Bible to shape corporate worship through liturgy, song and preaching. Sixth, both Sikhs and Christians claim to be monotheists, although how they understand that term differs. Seventh, both Jesus and Guru Nanak taught concern for humanity. Care for the needy is integral to both faiths. The key difference Cole and Sambhi outline is that Christians appear divided into many denominations whilst Sikhs appear unified. This fact is caveated by the greater age of Christianity, and the fact that for much of its early history, Christians were much more united. The fact that Punjabi is the language of Sikh devotion and the overwhelming majority of Sikhs live (or have ancestors who lived) in the Punjab is also relevant (1993, 6-9).

The bulk of Cole and Sambhi's book is divided into eleven chapters, each of which discusses an area of similarity and/or difference. I will consider each in turn.

Derived Religions

Jesus grew up Jewish, and as far as we know was an observant Jew all his life. Yet he challenged some of the norms of his day, and taught under his own authority. Guru Nanak was born into a Hindu family and whilst he rejected some aspects of Hinduism, did not turn away from it entirely. Indeed, as Cole and Sambhi state, nearly all of Guru Nanak's teachings can be found somewhere within Hindu thought.

Both could, perhaps, be thought of as attempting to reform the faith they were born into, but their approach was noticeably different. Jesus was vocally critical and confrontational; the record of his conversation with "the Jews" (or perhaps "Judeans") in John 8 and his condemnation of the Pharisees in Matthew 23 are clear examples of this. Guru Nanak, although equally critical of empty religiosity, was, by contrast, less likely to be drawn into arguments about the details of faith. Whilst Jesus condemned ritual purity as empty (Mark 7), Guru Nanak would not be drawn on matters of vegetarianism (AG 1289) or whether the dead should be buried or cremated (AG 466).

Cole and Sambhi suggest that the relationship between Christianity and Judaism has been ambivalent at best, and through much of history characterised by negative attitudes and persecution of Jews by Christians (1993, 18-19). Although they discuss the relationship between the two faiths as that of a parent and a child, this is misleading; modern rabbinical Judaism and modern Christianity are both children of Second Temple Judaism. A more apposite metaphor is that of siblings with common heritage, or as Rabbi Tony Bayfield suggests, parallel gardens (Bayfield 2017, 3).

Whilst Sikhi may distinguish itself from Hinduism, there are no condemnations of Hindu faith or practices within the writings of the Gurus. Cole and Sambhi note the condemnation of the caste system and criticism of the brahmins (1993, 20), to which could be added Guru Nanak's challenge and rebuke to all forms of empty ritual piety. In modern day India, Sikhs are at pains to distinguish themselves from Hindus, which manifests itself both in a political movement for a free Khalistan as well as in religious devotion and practice.

God

Christians and Sikhs are monotheists, but there are similarities and differences in how this is understood. Cole and

Sambhi suggest the most problematic point of disagreement concerns Christian belief in Jesus as God in human flesh, since Guru Nanak taught that the divine has no form or features (1993, 25). Jesus and the Gurus are discussed below, so nothing further will be said about this at present. A further issue is terminological; for ease of discussion, Cole and Sambhi retain "God" when discussing the Sikh perspective, but this term is potentially problematic in a western context due to the associated assumptions regarding gender; Christian language about God is invariably more masculine than feminine, but Sikhi does not recognise this distinction. The most concise summary of Guru Nanak's beliefs about *Waheguru* is found in the *mul mantar*, which has already been examined at some length above.

Cole and Sambhi point out that both Christians and Sikhs believe in natural theology, that is that the creation points towards a Creator. The Sikh understanding can, at times, appear monistic. For example Guru Nanak stated:

> God is the fish and the fisherman, the water and the net, the float of the net and the bait within it (AG 23, cited in Cole and Sambhi 1993, 27).

This reflects the Sikh belief that God's presence can be found in every experience and object. Thus,

> Seeing the marvel of God in nature, the mind is convinced. Through the Guru's word one realises that all that exists is God (AG 1043, cited in Cole and Sambhi 1993, 27).

But this does not mean that all created matter is itself divine. Rather the belief is that the individual soul can – and should – become united with the Primal Soul, *Brahman*.

Christians have a Trinitarian understanding of the divine; the Father is God, the Son is God and the Spirit is God. But there are not three Gods but one God. Jesus Christ reveals God the Father, who is the same God encountered in the Jewish scriptures and tradition, and the Holy Spirit continues God's work in the world, always consistent with what has been revealed of God by the Father and the Son.

Cole and Sambhi suggest that the most interesting and important area for discussion between Christians and Sikhs is the concept of the "Word." In the Hebrew Bible, God speaks creation in to being, and then speaks with those he has chosen, beginning with Adam and Eve, and Noah, Abraham, Moses, and then through his Prophets once the people are settled in the Promised Land. The understanding of "Word" is summarised by the Prophet Isaiah as follows:

> For as the rain and the snow come down from heaven,
>> and do not return there until they have watered the earth,
>
> making it bring forth and sprout,
>> giving seed to the sower and bread to the eater,
>
> so shall my word be that goes out from my mouth;
>> it shall not return to me empty,
>
> but it shall accomplish that which I purpose,
>> and succeed in the thing for which I sent it.
>> (Isaiah 55:10-11, NRSV).

The concept of *shabad* is equally rich in meaning, which has a significant history in all the Indian religions. For Sikhs, the Ultimate Reality is beyond human understanding and can only be known through divine self-revelation. Hence, they talk of *Akal Purakh*, the Being beyond time. The divine may become manifest as *Sat Guru*, the divine teacher and guide. The Sikh Gurus were inspired by *Sat Guru*, and so their function was to speak *shabad*, the divine word. Guru Nanak said: "The true creator, is known by means of the *shabad*" (AG 688, cited in Cole and Sambhi 31).

Cole and Sambhi explore the Christian and Sikh understanding of the nature of God. Both agree that humans can never fully understand God. As Guru Nanak said:

> The Lord is contained high up in the sky and down below in the nether regions too. How can I tell of the Lord? Make me understand this thing. Some rare people know what is the Name that is uttered in the mind, without the tongue. Without a doubt, words cease in such a state. That one alone understands on whom God's grace rests. (AG 1256, cited in Cole and Sambhi 1993, 34)

Cole and Sambhi suggest that Job 38-42, in which God speaks to Job, emphasising the gulf between Creator and created, is a suitable Biblical passage for comparison with this text.

For Sikhs, God has no form, and hence there is no scope for any attempt to portray a physical form of the divine. Christians might differ here, both with Sikhs and amongst themselves, with some, especially Roman Catholics, using pictures or statues of Jesus, Mary, and the saints as aids to prayer. The Orthodox Christian understanding of the production of icons as a form of prayer is also relevant to this discussion. But Christians would also want to point to the many condemnations of idolatry in their scriptures, especially amongst the Hebrew Prophets, of which Isaiah is perhaps the most vitriolic.

Christians and Sikhs agree that God is creator. For Sikhs, the term is *Karta Purakh*, and they believe that it was God's free choice to make the universe. As Guru Nanak states:

> God, self-created, assumed the Name (*Nam*). Secondly, God created nature and, seated within it, looked upon it with delight.
> You are the Giver and the Creator. As is your pleasure so you bestow and show mercy. You, knower of all, give and take life with a word. Abiding within your creation, you behold it with delight. (AG 463, cited in Cole and Sambhi 41)

In the Creation story in Genesis, God sees all he has made and "it was very good" (Genesis 1:31). Christians concur that God made the universe, and that it exists because of his providence and to point towards his majesty.

Both faiths also explain the existence of pain and suffering in the world with reference to the divine. For Christians, the devil and evil do exist, but only have limited power and ultimately have been defeated by Christ's crucifixion and resurrection. There are differences of belief and emphasis in relation to whether the devil and demons are real or not; those who deny they exist point particularly towards the risk of dualism, whereby good and evil are misunderstood to be on some sort of equal footing.

Within Sikhi, suffering and evil are the consequences of the mistaken belief that the world is permanent. People get attached to the material, and so are caught in *maya*, in delusion, and condemned to the cycle of rebirth. The story of Bhai Lalo, the poor but good man, in contrast with Malik Bhago, the rich but wicked man, is used by Sikhs to illustrate the power of *maya*.

Cole and Sambhi suggest that while the explanations may differ between Sikhs and Christians, devout people of both faiths would probably respond in a similar fashion to personal experiences of suffering. All might experience a greater sense of God's presence and love as they go through a difficult time, and rely primarily on their relationship of faith with the divine, rather than on neat and tidy theological explanations, in order to get themselves through (1993, 44).

Within Sikh teaching, God is beyond the categories of male and female. Thus, Guru Nanak explains that "The wise and beauteous Being (*purakh*) is neither a man nor a woman nor a bird" (AG 1010, cited in Cole and Sambhi 1993, 45). Such categorisations are limited to the creation, and are *maya*, in the sense that they have their place and use but can also become distractions and attachments that keep us from the divine. At the close of worship, a Sikh might say of the divine, "You are my mother and father, we are your children(AG 268) or "You are my father, you are my mother, you are my kinsman, you are my brother" (AG 103) (Cole and Sambhi 1993, 45-46).

Whilst Christians would affirm that God is beyond gender, it is nevertheless true that there are very few examples of female language used in reference to the divine. Jesus does refer to himself as a mother hen (Matthew 23:37), but this is one of only a very few direct examples. There are a few within the Hebrew Scriptures, including:

> You were unmindful of the Rock that bore you;
> > you forgot the God who gave you birth.
> > (Deuteronomy 32:18, NRSV).

> As a mother comforts her child,
> > so I will comfort you;
> > you shall be comforted in Jerusalem. (Isaiah 66:13, NRSV).

But these are the exceptions that prove the rule that within Christian scripture, the divine is addressed primarily as male.

The final area that Cole and Sambhi discuss is that of God as ruler of history. For Christians history is teleological, with a beginning and working towards an end point, when God will judge the world. The closing chapters of Revelation, the final book of the Bible, discuss this in colourful pictorial language. Other texts, notably the letters of Paul and Peter, also emphasise the importance of living with the expectation that God will judge the world. Devout Christians pray "your kingdom come, your will be done," every time they say the Lord's Prayer, and so state their belief in the divine control of history. Cole and Sambhi refer to the *Babur bani*, four verses in the Guru Granth Sahib where Guru Nanak refers to the Mughal Babur's invasion of northern India between 1520 and 1526. The second verse reads:

> The wealth and sensual beauty which had intoxicated them became their enemies. The command was given to the messengers of Death to strip them of their honour and carry them off. If it seems good to you, you give glory, if it pleases you, you give punishment. If they had taken time to think would they have received punishment? But the rulers paid no heed, instead they passed their time in merry making. Now Babur's authority has been established the princes starve. (AG 417, cited in Cole and Sambhi 1993, 48)

The first and third verses are similar and might reflect eyewitness accounts of the invasion. But, as Cole and Sambhi note, the underlying assumption is of divine control over history. A similar thought is found in the writing of the Hebrew Prophets, especially the descriptions of the judgement visited on and by the nations.

Jesus and the Gurus

The focus of Cole and Sambhi's discussion is on how Jesus and the Gurus mediate divine revelation. Jesus both preached God's Word and was himself the Word; Gurus were messengers through whom God's Word was revealed. Whilst this may, on the surface, appear to indicate both concepts are similar, the Christian belief in the Incarnation of Jesus constitutes a major difference between the two faiths. For Sikhs *Akal Purakh* is *nirguna*, without physical form. Moreover, Sikhs believe that *Waheguru* to be all-powerful, creator and sustainer of all; human beings are powerless before him. Cole and Sambhi propose that whilst the Gurus do not address the topic of incarnation directly, they do respond to the Hindu notion of avatar, in particular the understanding of Krishna as an avatar of Vishnu as taught in the Bhagavad Gita. Whilst Krishna's *lila* (play) is very different from the Incarnation of Christ, nevertheless both are anathema to a Sikh understanding of the divine.

Christians believe in miracles, and the New Testament teaches that the miraculous acts of Jesus are signs pointing towards his divinity. Sikhs do not accept miracles in the sense of wonder working. Indeed, when Guru Nanak was asked to prove his authority through performing miracles, he replied to the yogis who questioned him saying:

> I have nothing to exhibit, no supernatural powers to display, for I depend on nothing but the holy congregation(*sangat*) and the Word (*shabad*). (Bhai Gurdas, Var I, pauri 42, cited in Cole and Sambhi 1993, 54).

Performing miracles for praise or personal profit is against the teaching of both faiths. Cole and Sambhi suggest that Sikhs would see Jesus' miracles as like the "miracle" of *shabad* that was spoken by the Gurus (1993, 55).

Cole and Sambhi point out that the Sikh ambivalence towards the concept of incarnation is really a rejection of Hindu, not Christian teaching. They recognise the range of New Testament teaching on the nature of Jesus' Incarnation and propose that John's use of the *Logos*, the Word is the one that would have the greatest resonance and provide the most fruitful avenues for discussion. When a Sikh reads the opening verses of John's Gospel, perhaps the following passages would come to mind:

> The *Gurbani* (Word) is Guru and the Guru is the *Gurbani* (AG 982, Guru Ram Das).

> The Guru's Word abides with my soul (AG 679, Guru Arjan).

> The *Gurbani* is the divine light in this world. Through grace it comes to abide in the minds of mortals (AG 67, Guru Amar Das).

> O disciples of the True Guru, know that the Word of the Guru is perfectly true; God, the Creator, causes it to be uttered (AG 308, Guru Ram Das, all quotes from Cole and Sambhi 1993, 57).

What it means for the Word to be in the world, the form it takes and the impact the Word has, therefore provides a fruitful avenue for dialogue.

A further area of discussion is the concept of suffering. For Christians, the so-called "problem of evil" finds its solution in the death of Christ on the Cross. Whilst they may struggle to articulate clearly what it signifies, the crucifixion of Jesus, a completely innocent man, was part of God's plan for the redemption of the world. The divine victory is signified by Jesus' resurrection, which points also towards the defeat of death. Sikhs regard much suffering to be the result of *maya*, delusion and false attachment. There is no concept of evil as an independent entity; Guru Nanak taught that rather than debate the origin of evil, one must seek the solution:

> Do not delay in practising righteousness, but think before committing evil. Hold fast to God, and forsake greed. Seek the protection of God's holy people to wash away impurity so that you may become righteous (AG 1352, cited in Cole and Sambhi 1993, 65-66).

Suffering does not exist to drive people to God; rather suffering is real but can only be escaped from through union with the divine.

Spiritual Liberation and Salvation

Christian doctrine teaches that human beings are estranged from God as a result of Adam's disobedience. In Genesis 2:17, God places Adam and Eve in the Garden of Eden and gives them everything there to eat, except for the fruit of one tree. But they are tempted by the Serpent, who is Satan, and eat from the tree of knowledge (Genesis 3:6). They are therefore cursed; their lives will now be characterised by pain and suffering, and they are expelled from the Garden(Genesis 3:22-24). Whilst Judaism does not teach that all humanity were condemned because of this one action, Christianity does. This is what is sometimes termed "original sin." As Paul puts it in his letter to the Church in Corinth:

> For since death came through a human being, the resurrection of the dead has also come

> through a human being; for as all die in Adam, so all will be made alive in Christ (1 Corinthians 15:21-22, NRSV).

Jesus himself spoke of his mission to suffer and die for the sins of others, explaining that he "came not to be served but to serve, and to give his life a ransom for many" (Mark 10:45, NRSV). Whilst we can point towards political and religious motives for Jesus' trial and subsequent execution, the primary point, for Christians, is theological. Human beings are, Christians believe, in a predicament from which they cannot extricate themselves. It is only through Christ's sacrifice on the cross that healing and restoration are possible.

The Sikh understanding of humanity is very different. Rather than discuss sin, the focus is on ignorance and failure to realise potential. As Guru Nanak put it, "God is hidden in every heart; the Lord illuminates every heart" (AG 579, cited in Cole and Sambhi 1993, 74). Thus in the Sikh worldview, the problem is *man*, not sin. Cole and Sambhi explain this Punjabi word is hard to translate, but it might mean "mind," "soul," or "heart." For those who are unenlightened, *man* is an unreliable guide. Guru Nanak warned:

> The *man* is unsteady, it does not know the way. One who puts his trust in his own *man* is as one befouled; he does not recognise the Word (*shabad*) (AG 415, cited in Cole and Sambhi 1993, 75).

The human predicament is caused by *haumai*, self-reliance, and compounded by *maya*, an incorrect interpretation of creation as dualistic, believing that things exist independently, rather than because *Akal Purakh* wills them to exist. If people will only recognise that creation exists for the glory of the divine, then they can be lifted to spiritual liberation.

SIKHISM AND CHRISTIANITY

Whilst there are clear differences in the understanding of the human condition, both Sikhs and Christians focus on divine grace. Cole and Sambhi contrast an extract from Paul's letter to the Ephesians with a saying of Guru Nanak:

> For by grace you have been saved through faith, and this is not your own doing; it is the gift of God—not the result of works, so that no one may boast. (Ephesians 2:8-9, NRSV).

> Without (God's) grace, Nanak says, no one is liberated; if God is gracious God is called to mind, the soul is softened and one becomes absorbed in the love of God. The soul is made one with the Supreme Soul. (AG 661, cited in Cole and Sambhi 1993, 82).

As Cole and Sambhi explain, both Paul and Guru Nanak are reacting against teaching that liberation or salvation can be attained through human effort, whether that is following one's *dharma* as a Hindu, or keeping the Torah as an observant Jew. This emphasis on grace can lead to spiritual laziness, hence both faiths also teach of the importance of a changed way of life. One may be saved by grace, but one is expected to respond with gratitude characterised by selfless service of others (Cole and Sambhi 1993, 82-83).

The final area of discussion is that adherents of both faiths expect to encounter the divine both in personal prayer and in public worship. Christians believe that where two or three gather in God's name, Jesus is present with them (Matthew 18:20) and similarly, Sikhs are taught that God's essence "is obtained in the congregation of the holy(*sat sangat*) (AG 598, cited in Cole and Sambhi 1993, 85).

The Scriptures

Both Christianity and Sikhi value scripture highly, but in different ways. Christians vary as to the way they use scripture in personal devotion and corporate worship. By contrast, for Sikhs the Guru Granth Sahib is always the focal point of worship. The term "gurdwara" refers to a building in which the Guru Granth Sahib is present. It is not the "house" of the divine, but the gateway to the Guru Granth Sahib.

Christianity has appropriated and reinterpreted the Hebrew Bible, finding within in numerous pointers and prophecies of Jesus as the Messiah. Guru Nanak had a different attitude towards Hindu sacred texts; although qualified by his caste status as a *khatri Vaishya* to study the Vedas, he was not permitted to teach them. Moreover, as Cole and Sambhi explain, Guru Nanak rejected the idea of a priestly caste and also of scripture as a closed corpus of revelation(1993, 90-91).

The Vedas are recognised as having value. Guru Nanak wrote:

> *Nam* is the support of the worlds and universes,
> *Nam* is the support of the smritis, vedas and puranas (AG 284, cited in Cole and Sambhi 1993, 91).

The Guru Granth Sahib makes no judgement about the Quran, but Guru Nanak described a Muslim as "one who removes impurity by reading and acting upon what he reads," thus becoming acceptable towards God (AG 662, cited in Cole and Sambhi 1993, 92).

The Sikh and Christian sacred texts were both complied by the generations subsequent to the founder. The texts that eventually became the New Testament began to be written in the decades after Jesus' death; Paul's letters are some of the earlier compositions and predate the four canonical Gospels. The final form of the New Testament was not agreed for several hundred years. It was the fifth Guru, Arjan, who began the task of collating and organising the compositions of the first four Gurus. Cole and Sambhi suggest there were two motivations for this: to distinguish and preserve orthodox texts and to provide the growing Sikh community with resources to facilitate their worship.

It is important to recognise that the Guru Granth Sahib does not just contain Sikh texts; it includes compositions from Muslims and Hindus as well, which were gathered – and responded to – by Guru Nanak. To give one example, Kabir writes:

> Impurity attaches to whatever we do. Even our kitchen is impure. All devices for avoiding it only increase our bondage. Rare are those who realise the way of liberation. Says Kabir: impurity does not attach itself to those who contemplate the Lord in their hearts (AG 331).

To this Guru Nanak responds:

> How may impurity be removed when even our kitchen is impure? Says Nanak: such impurity is only washed away by enlightenment (AG 472, cited in Cole and Sambhi 1993, 97).

Other examples could also be given, but the point is clear. Both Sikhs and Christians use their sacred texts within worship, the topic to which we now turn.

Worship

The purpose of worship is to glorify God. As Guru Nanak put it:

> What should I ask and what should I be heard uttering except that I hunger and thirst for your sight! (AG 762, cited in Cole and Sambhi 1993, 117).

Equally, in the Psalms we read

> My soul longs, indeed it faints
>   for the courts of the Lord;
> my heart and my flesh sing for joy
>   to the living God. (Psalm 84:2, NRSV).

Both Sikhs and Christians worship out of a desire to connect with and celebrate the Creator.

Christians are sometimes confused as to the status and purpose of *karah prashad* and whether it is somehow equivalent to Holy Communion. Cole and Sambhi explain that the purpose of distributing *karah prashad* is simply to remind Sikhs of their duty to provide food for the needy, as well as reminding them that they are all equal, and that Sikhs reject any caste-based discrimination. *Karah prashad* is a pudding made of wholemeal flour, sugar and clarified butter (*ghee*), that is blessed as it is produced, through recitation of verses of the Gurus. But it does not have the status that the Eucharist has in most Christian denominations. In a similar way, *langar,* the practice of sharing a meal together and the distribution of food to whoever turns up should not be equated with the Eucharist (1993, 124-25).

Whilst nearly all Christian denominations ordain ministers, to lead worship and administer sacraments, but there is no similar practice in the Sikh faith. Cole and Sambhi identify two functionary roles. First, that of *granthi*, the one who reads from the Guru Granth Sahib as required, whether in public worship or a more private ceremony such as a wedding. Some *granthis* may have other responsibilities, including the care of the gurdwara, education of the young and so forth. Second, the *ragis*, musicians who lead and accompany the singing of *kirtans* in worship. These may be professionals or amateurs as the context and occasion demands (1993, 127-28).

Personal devotion

Cole and Sambhi open their discussion of personal devotion by observing that

> Christians and Sikhs have usually only a slight awareness of what actually happens in the homes of their co-religionists, let alone behind the closed doors of people of another faith (1993, 139).

Discussion of private spiritual practices is a highly personal conversation, and it may be difficult for people to feel sufficiently safe to disclose the intimate details of their relationship with the divine. An in-person dialogue may reach the point where lived religion is a natural topic of conversation, but for the purpose of this overview, three generic observations will suffice.

First, both faiths emphasise the importance of beginning the day with prayer. Guru Nanak said:

> A godly person who contemplates the Name through the Word, in the early morning, shedding love of the world, wins, while the world loses (AG 1330, cited in Cole and Sambhi 1993, 140).

Similarly, Jesus instructed his followers to pray in secret (Matthew 6:6), and set an example of going away by himself early in the morning to pray (for example Mark 1:35).

Second, adherents of both faith traditions may use aids to concentration and prayer, for example prayer beads such as a rosary, used by some Christians or a *mala*, a circle made of wool with 108 knots used by some Sikhs.

Third, and most crucially, the diversity of practice is so considerable, and unknowable, that without considerable personal disclosure it is hard to say much with any confidence about what "all Sikhs" or "all Christians" do in terms of personal devotions. A more productive approach is to ask those known to you how they nurture their relationship with the divine.

Ceremonies

The main ceremonies that Cole and Sambhi discuss are those of initiation, marriage, and death. For Christians, baptism is the agreed initiation ceremony, although there are differences between denominations as to whether it should be administered to babies, adults, or both. Those who baptise babies often also have a secondary ritual, of confirmation, which normally takes place in teenage years or early adulthood. There are two denominations that do not baptise; the Salvation Army and the Society of Friends (Quakers), who believe that outward sacraments are not necessary, as it is the Holy Spirit who baptises. For those who do perform the ritual, it is seen as a sign of sins being washed away and an opportunity to make a declaration of public allegiance to Christ.

Sikhs do hold a naming ceremony, which has already been explained. It must be noted that this is different from baptism, which is not a ceremony of naming, but of welcome into the Christian Church. The origins of the Sikh ceremony of *amrit sanskar* are discussed elsewhere and will not be repeated here. The main point to note is that this is always performed for those of sufficient maturity, not for babies or young children.

Both Sikhs and Christians prefer to be married in their place of worship, in the presence of God. Some Christians, notably the Roman Catholic and Orthodox Churches, regard marriage as a sacrament. All hold the ceremony to be important, and many Christian marriage liturgies refer to Jesus attending a wedding at Cana in Galilee (John 2). Christians also recognise celibacy as a calling, noting that both Jesus and Paul were not married.

Sikhs do not teach the importance of asceticism. The Guru taught that

> Contemplation of the True Name brings that illumination which enables one to live detached in the midst of evil. Such is the distinctive greatness of the True Guru through whose grace and guidance salvation can be attained even though one may be surrounded by one's wife and children (AG 661, cited in Cole and Sambhi 1993, 157).

The point is not that marriage is bad, but rather that marriage has consequences; those who are married have responsibilities to fulfil to spouse and children and this can make spiritual marriage to the divine that bit more challenging.

Christians believe in the resurrection of the dead, and that Jesus is the "first fruits" of the resurrection, pointing towards what will one day be enjoyed by all his followers. Sikhs believe that those who attain liberation are freed from the possibility of re-birth and become united with the divine upon death. Thus for people of both faiths, bereavement is both devastating but also hopeful.

Sikhs prepare the deceased for cremation by dressing them with the five Ks, and taking the body to the cremation ground. Prayers and hymns are sung, the body placed on the pyre, the *Ardas* is recited, and the pyre is lit. Once it is sufficiently alight, further prayers are said and at the right moment, the mourners return to the relatives' home, where they are thanked for attending. Christians vary as to whether they emphasise burial or cremation. Some emphasise the former, and historically burial was felt necessary for the resurrection of the dead (but perhaps also to distinguish Christianity from pagan practices). The most significant difference in practice between the two faiths is that while Christians will bring the coffin containing the deceased into church, and even hold a vigil the night before a funeral with the coffin, Sikhs would never take a corpse into a gurdwara.

Authority

Both Jesus and Guru Nanak operated under their own authority. When he taught his Sermon on the Mount, Jesus repeated the refrain "You have heard it said ... But I say to you..." When asked about his sect and authority, Guru Nanak replied: "I have come from God and shall go wherever God's will directs me" (AG 938, cited in Cole and Sambhi 1993, 162).

Their followers have interpreted this authority in different ways. Some denominations of Christianity are hierarchical; Roman Catholics for example claim that the Pope is the spiritual descendant of a line reaching back to the Apostle Peter. Other Christian groups, whilst having a clear leadership structure, would not make such claims. For Sikhs, the authority is ultimately in the Guru Granth Sahib, the living

Guru. When Guru Gobind Singh initiated the first five members at Vaisakhi in 1699, he also established the authority of the Khalsa Panth. Thus, Cole and Sambhi suggest, "authority in Sikhism lies in the Khalsa Panth gathered around the Guru Granth Sahib" (1993, 166). Within a gurdwara, there will be a leadership committee, but the ultimate decision-making body is the whole *sangat*. There is no organisation that can speak with definitive authority for all Sikhs. There are five *takhts*, or seats of authority, based in five gurdwaras that have special status within Sikhi. These are *Akal Takht*, based at the Golden Temple in Amritsar; *Takht Sri Keshgarh*, based at Anandpur, the birthplace of the Khalsa; *Takht Sri Damdama*, in the village of Talwindi Sabo, where Guru Gobind Singh compiled the final edition of the Guru Granth Sahib; *Takht Sri Patna*, where Guru Gobind Singh was born, and Guru Nanak visited; and *Takht Sri Hazur*, at Nanded, where Guru Gobind Singh's body was cremated.

In their discussion of authority, Cole and Sambhi tackle the question of orthodoxy, examining how one can determine if a person is, for example, a Sikh or a Christian. They conclude that a balance of subjectivity and objectivity is required; there are certain objective facts (belief in the ten Gurus, or the divinity of Christ, for example), but at the same time it is also a subjective choice, a decision to identify oneself in a particular way, for example as a follower of Jesus or of Guru Nanak.

Ethics

Christians focus their ethical teaching on the two great commandments; to love God with all your heart, soul, mind and strength, and to love one's neighbour as oneself (Luke 10:27). Sikhs speak of Bhai Kanaya, who followed Guru Gobind Singh, and who, during a battle between the Sikhs and Mughals, treated the wounded, regardless of who they were. This principle of *seva*, service for all, is the highest virtue for a Sikh.

Cole and Sambhi point out that both faiths began in positions of relative weakness; as such they could not shape the ethics of society, but could command their own followers to attain high ethical standards. Perhaps this decision, to not confront wider society, but simply to challenge through a greater moral stance, contributed to the growth of each faith during their formative years. A case can therefore be made that ethical focus was, during these early years, primarily on individuals and families (1993, 180-82).

Perhaps the biggest difference between Sikh and Christian ethics is the place given to women. In first-century Greco-Roman society women simply did not have the status men enjoyed. Although Christianity challenged this to an extent, arguably Guru Nanak's acceptance of female disciples and his rebuke of any lack of respect for women went further (Cole and Sambhi 1993, 183-84).

Another significant difference relates to the possibility of pacifism. Whilst both Sikh and Christian ethical codes have criteria for when warfare is justifiable, there is no tradition of pacifism, complete rejection of warfare, within Sikhi. Indeed, members of the Khalsa are taught they should take up arms to defend righteousness where there is oppression and tyranny.

Third, while some individual Christians are comfortable with the use of alcohol and tobacco (and perhaps other drugs as well, for example for birth control), the same cannot be said of Sikhs. Alcohol and tobacco, and any other intoxicant, are all forbidden to initiated Sikhs, and there is teaching that any form of birth control is a denial of karma. Ultimately all ethical decisions remain the purview of individual conscience; even if there is a particular ethical stance held by some in religious authority, that does not necessarily mean everyone who identifies as a follower of that faith conforms to those standards.

Attitudes to other religions

The final topic Cole and Sambhi discuss is the view of other religious traditions. Christians, they suggest, hold one of three attitudes: first, that other religions have no salvific value, and that salvation is through Jesus alone. Second, that Christianity is simply one religion amongst many, equally valid, paths up the mountain towards God. Third, what they describe as an "intermediate" position, which sees the Holy Spirit at work in other faiths, but "nevertheless safeguards belief in the 'finality of Christ', to use a popular phrase" (1993, 193).

Sikhi is founded on acceptance of other religions as authentic. After all, Guru Nanak's musician Mardana was a Muslim. Cole and Sambhi cite teachings that show his acceptance of the validity of other faiths. For example, on Islam, the Guru said:

> There are five prayers, five times and five names given to them. Let truthfulness be the first, honest living the second, charity in God's name be the third, purity of mind and good intention the fourth. The fifth the praise and adoration of God. Let good deeds be your article of faith. Thus will you be called a true Muslim (AG 141, cited in Cole and Sambhi 1993, 195).

And on Hinduism, to give a single example from many positive texts, Guru Nanak said:

> He who holds fast to the Lord's Name and causes others to repeat it; Nanak says such a *Vaishnava* obtains supreme liberation (AG 274, cited in Cole and Sambhi 1993, 196).

This does not mean that Guru Nanak was uncritical of Hindus or Muslims; rather that he had no interest in persuading them to become Sikhs. He was simply urging them to be more aware and spiritually active Hindus and Muslims, to live out their own faith in such a way as to make a significant difference in the world. Kaur Singh suggests that Guru Nanak's approach is Socratic; focused on questions and discussion, on mutual learning and development, without a rigid system of doctrines that must be adhered to, people are invited to enhance their powers of reasoning and become whom they truly are (2011, 20).

Cole and Sambhi conclude with an affirmation of the Council of Churches for Britain and Ireland's four conditions for dialogue. These are to first, meet to dialogue, with a readiness to listen more than to speak, to learn rather than to witness. Second, to develop mutual understanding and trust, taking time, not rushing, or forcing the issue. Third, dialogue may make it possible to work together for the community, but only if this comes naturally. Fourth, dialogue can become the means of mutual witness, once a relationship is sufficiently strong then honest sharing of faith is natural and normal (1993, 202-3).

Chapter 10

Learning to Live Well Together

My aim in writing this book was two-fold. First, to increase my understanding of and appreciation for Sikhi, and second, to contrast my own Christian faith with my enhanced understanding of what Sikhs believe. I hope that the result is one that others can use for the same purpose, whether they are Sikh, Christian or indeed of any other faith or belief perspective. We live in a complex, contested pluralist world, where our main hope of peaceful co-existence lies in individuals and groups making the effort to build relationships of trust and cooperation with people who see the world very differently from themselves.

In chapter one I introduced the book, and gave a brief overview of Guru Nanak's life and the core teachings of Sikhi. Chapters two and three examined specific texts from the Guru Granth Sahib in more detail, first *Japji* and then the *mul mantar*. The teaching found there was read subjectively in the light of my own Christian faith, with the intention of sharing my own thoughts to aid others entry into dialogue. Chapter four introduced the *janam sakhi* literature, contrasting the attitude of different scholars. Chapters five to seven then explored the *janam sakhis* in more detail, examining some of the most popular stories and contrasting the with incidents in Jesus' life, as well as in a few cases other stories in the Hebrew Scriptures and apocryphal gospels. Chapters eight and nine focused on dialogue between Christians and Sikhs, both records of conversations, primarily in Parry's work, as well as written discussions, notably those of Gopal Singh and Cole and Sambhi.

One key point to recognise from Parry's work is that the history of the sub-continent of India continues to impact relationships between Sikhs and Christians today. Parry's point about "suspicion and concern" is a reminder that the way Christian missionaries mistreated Sikhs in the past remains a barrier to conversation today. If you are establishing a dialogue, it is important to be clear on the intentions, boundaries and scope of any such meeting. Proceed with caution, for all people are made in the image of God and are deserving of respect and care in how they are treated.

That is not to say we should avoid meeting with each other; far from it. The previous two chapters have indicated a rich field of topics for discussion, including but by no means limited to exploration of *japji* and the Lord's prayer; understandings of *logos* and *shabad*, that is, what is meant by Word; how we experience divine grace in our lives; what it is to live out our faith today, including how we practice personal devotions; and the lives (and deaths) of the founders of our faiths.

At the St Philip's Centre, of which I am director, we believe that despite all the disputes and divisions that trouble our world, we can learn to live well together. We aim to facilitate genuine encounters between people who see the world differently. As a result of those encounters, we hope people will understand each other better, without necessarily agreeing with each other. Understanding can lead to relationships of trust developing, and as a result, people cooperating for the good of all. The purpose of this book is to make suggestions for dialogue, helping people genuinely listen to each other. It is written as a stimulus for discussion, and does not claim to be a definitive expression of either Sikhi or Christianity. My hope and prayer is that as a result of reading it, people will learn how to live well together.

Bibliography

Ahluwalia, Jasbir Singh. (1999). *The Doctrine and Dynamics of Sikhism*. Patiala: Publication Bureau of Punjabi University.

Ahluwalia, Jasbir Singh. (2001). *Doctrinal Aspects of Sikhism and Other Essays*. Patiala: Publication Bureau of Punjabi University.

Bayfield, Tony. (2017). *Deep Calls to Deep: Transforming Conversations between Jews and Christians*. London: SCM Press.

Cole, Owen. (1982). *The Guru in Sikhism*. London: Darton, Longman and Todd.

Cole, Owen and Piara Singh Sambhi. (1993). *Sikhism and Christianity: A comparative study*. London: MacMillan.

Cole, Owen and Piara Singh Sambhi. (2006). *The Sikhs: Their Religious Beliefs and Practices*. Brighton: Sussex Academic Press.

Jakobsh, Doris R. (2012). *Sikhism: Dimensions of Asian Spirituality*. Honolulu: University of Hawai'i Press.

Jaspal, Rusi and Opinderjit Kaur Takhar. (2016). "Caste and Identity Processes among British Sikhs in the Midlands" *Sikh Formations: Religion, Culture, Theory*. 12 (1) 87-102.

Johnson, Toby. (2015). *Living and Learning with Guru Nanak: Participation and Pedagogy in the Janam-Sakhi Narratives*.

Unpublished PhD dissertation Permalink: https://escholarship.org/uc/item/8xt8v3dm.

Kaur Singh, Nikky-Guninder. (1995). *Hymns of the Sikh Gurus*. London: Penguin Books.

Kaur Singh, Nikky-Guninder. (2011). *Sikhism: An Introduction*. London: I. B. Tauris.

LeDonne, Anthony and Larry Behrendt. (2017). *Sacred Dissonance: The Blessing of Difference in Jewish-Christian Dialogue*. Peabody: Hendrickson

Mandair, Arvind-Pal Singh. (2013). *Sikhism: A Guide for the Perplexed*. London: Bloomsbury.

Massey, James. (1991). *The Doctrine of Ultimate Reality in Sikh Religion: A Study of Guru Nanak's Hymns in the Adi Granth*. New Delhi: Manohar Publishers.

Massey, James. (2010). *A Contemporary Look at Sikh Religion: Essays on Scripture, Identity, Creation, Spirituality, Charity and Interfaith Dialogue*. New Delhi: Manohar Publishers.

McLeod, W. H. (1968). *Guru Nanak and the Sikh Religion*. Oxford: Clarendon Press.

McLeod, W. H. (1984). *Textual Sources for the Study of Sikhism*. Manchester: Manchester University Press.

Murphy, Anne. (2016). "Representations of Sikh History" in Singh, Pashura and Louis E. French. *The Oxford Handbook of Sikh Studies*. Oxford: Oxford University Press, pp.94-108.

Oberoi, Harjot. (2000). *Sikhism* in Coward, Harold. *Experiencing Scripture in World Religions*. Maryknoll: Orbis Books, pp.113-37.

Parry, John. (2009). *The Word of God is Not Bound*. Bangalore: Centre for Contemporary Christianity.

Phillips, J. B. (2004) *Your God is Too Small*. New York: Touchstone Books.

Bibliography

Shackle, Christopher and Arvin-pal Singh Mandair. (2005). *Teachings of the Sikh Gurus: Selections from the Sikh Scriptures.* London: Routledge.

Shackle, Christopher. (2016). "Survey of Literature in the Sikh Tradition" in Singh, Pashura and Louis E. French. *The Oxford Handbook of Sikh Studies.* Oxford: Oxford University Press, pp.109-24.

Shapiro, Michael C. (2016). "Linguistic and Philological Approaches to Sacred Sikh Literature" in Singh, Pashura and Louis E. French. *The Oxford Handbook of Sikh Studies.* Oxford: Oxford University Press, pp.212-225.

Singh, Gopal. (1990). *The Man Who Never Died.* Honesdale: The Himalayan International Institute of Yoga Science and Philosophy of the USA.

Singh, Kirpal. (2004). *Janamsakhi Tradition: An Analytical Study.* Amritsar: Singh Brothers.

Singh, Pashaura. (2016). "An Overview of Sikh History" in Singh, Pashura and Louis E. French. *The Oxford Handbook of Sikh Studies.* Oxford: Oxford University Press, pp.19-34.

Sondhi, S. P. (2002). *Grace of God and Guru in Sikh Philosophy.* Delhi: Global Vision Publishing House.

Sutton, Nicholas. (2016). *Bhagavad-Gita* .Oxford: Oxford Centre for Hindu Studies.

Wright, Nicholas T. (1993). *The New Testament and the People of God.* (London: SPCK).

Wright, Nicholas T. (1996). *Jesus and the Victory of God.* (London: SPCK).

Wright, Nicholas T. (2003). *The Resurrection of the Son of God.* (Minneapolis: Fortress Press).

www.ingramcontent.com/pod-product-compliance
Lightning Source LLC
Chambersburg PA
CBHW061318040426
42444CB00011B/2698